KU-167-815

Embroidery
Stitches
STEP BY STEP

WITHDRAWN FROM STOCK

Embroidery Stitches

STEP BY STEP

· · · · · · · ◆ · · · · · · ·

Lucinda Ganderton

Penguin Random House

Dedicated to the memory of
Mary Josephine Ganderton,
my mother and my inspiration

Senior Editor: Mary Lindsay
Senior Art Editor: Sarah Hall
Production Controller: Michelle Thomas
DTP Designer: Jason Little
Managing Editors: Stephanie Jackson, Jonathan
Metcalf
Managing Art Editor: Nigel Duffield
Jacket Designer: Nicola Powling

Produced by
C&B Packaging Ltd
London House, Great Eastern Wharf
Parkgate Road, London SW11 4NQ

Managing Editor: Kate Yeates
Editor: Heather Dewhurst
Art Director: Roger Bristow
Art Editor: Helen Collins
Designers: Suzanne Metcalfe-Megginson, Bill Mason
Photography: Sampson Lloyd

First published in Great Britain in 1999
This edition published in Great Britain in 2015 by
Dorling Kindersley Limited,
80 Strand, London, WC2R 0RL

Copyright © 1999, 2015 Dorling Kindersley Limited
A Penguin Random House Company
Text copyright © 1999, 2015 Lucinda Ganderton
The moral right of Lucinda Ganderton to be
identified as the author of this book has
been asserted.
10 9 8 7 6 5 4 3
006-280243-June/2015

All rights reserved.
No part of this publication may be reproduced,
stored in or introduced into a retrieval system, or
transmitted, in any form, or by any means
(electronic, mechanical, photocopying, recording, or
otherwise) without the prior written permission of
the copyright owner.

A CIP catalogue record for this book
is available from the British Library.

ISBN: 978-0-2412-0139-8

Printed and bound in China.
Colour reproduction by Altaimage UK.

All images © Dorling Kindersley Limited
For further information see: www.dkimages.com

A WORLD OF IDEAS:
SEE ALL THERE IS TO KNOW

CONTENTS

Introduction

THE ART OF embroidery has been defined simply as the ornamentation of textiles with decorative stitchery. It is an ancient craft which encompasses a wealth of history, and the same stitches are used by embroiderers throughout the world. They provide an international vocabulary that crosses the boundaries of land and time. Local patterns, designs, and ways of working vary from place to place, but the actual stitch techniques do not. The language of stitches is infinitely adaptable. It is being constantly reinterpreted by contemporary stitchers, who produce their new work as part of a continuing tradition.

INTERNATIONAL HERITAGE

Sewing was once an essential part of daily life for most women, and some men. Before mass production, many clothes and items of domestic furnishing had to be made at home and embroidery evolved as a means of decorating and personalising the plain needlework used for household linens and garments.

People in different countries concentrated on their own particular aspects of embroidery and names such as Bokhara couching, Antwerp edging, Portuguese border, and Algerian eye reflect the international aspect of the stitches they worked with. Creative concepts are always interchanged; patterns and ideas have travelled and developed throughout the world. German immigrants in Pennsylvania, for example, had to adapt their own traditional dense cross stitch patterns to outline-based designs, because of the shortage of embroidery threads in the New World.

PORTRAIT OF A LADY
Fine silk threads in a subtle range of natural dyes were used to embroider this eighteenth century picture. Layers of straight stitches have been worked in many directions to build up the image.

FLORAL BORDER
Long decorative bands, like this tent stitch pattern in bright Berlin wools, were worked by Victorian ladies and used to adorn cushions and throws.

TYPES OF STITCH

Embroidery stitches are worked on fabric, while needlepoint stitches are sewn on to canvas. Although there are hundreds of individual stitches used for both these techniques, they can be classified into just four groups, according to the way they are constructed: flat stitches which lie on the surface of the fabric; looped stitches, where one stitch is anchored by another; knotted stitches in which the thread is twisted back on itself to form a raised stitch, and openwork stitches which create a regular pattern of spaces, integrating the thread with the background fabric.

USING STITCHES

The various stitches within these four groups are endlessly adaptable and can be used in many ways, depending on the effect required. They can outline a design, be worked closely together so that they conceal the fabric completely, or be spaced further apart to allow the background to show through. Others may be used singly, repeated in rows, or stitched in a solid line.

Certain stitches were developed for particular reasons. Gold thread is costly and too thick to pass easily through the fabric, so couching stitch was used to anchor it to the fabric with small stitches in fine thread. Turkey stitch evolved as an imitation of the cut pile of a rug, and insertion stitches were used as a means of joining two pieces of fabric.

One single stitch may be used throughout a piece of work. Rows of tent and cross stitches are used to create both samplers and embroidered pictures, while straight stitch can be used randomly like a painter's brushstrokes to build up a textured, three-dimensional surface. It is when the patterns and shapes of the various stitches are combined, however, that their full potential is realised.

STITCH NAMES

For many centuries, knowledge of embroidery stitches was handed down as part of the wider folk tradition of needlecraft. It was not until 1631, when *The Needle's Excellency* was printed, that their names began to be formalised in Europe. This was a book of patterns,

COUNTRY GARDEN
This characteristic transfer design from the 1930s features plants worked with French knots, link, fly, and buttonhole stitches, and outlines in stem stitch.

GOLD SLIPPER
Straight stitch flowers in silk floss have been combined with gold thread couched in a swirling pattern to decorate this beautiful nineteenth century slipper top.

not a practical manual, and there were no working diagrams or
stitch illustrations. Some of the stitches listed – Fern-stitch,
Chain-stitch, Back-stitch and the Crosse-stitch – are still in
general use. Various other names were adopted over the
following centuries. Some described the way in which the
actual stitches were made, for example, twisted insertion and
back stitch trellis. Others, such as cushion stitch, ladder stitch,
window filling, and rope stitch, were named after the objects of
daily life that they resembled. Still more were inspired by the
surroundings of the natural world: star, wave, cloud, feather,
coral, leaf, petal, and wheatear stitches.

Needlework was not valued as a separate area of study until
the late nineteenth century. Under the influence of the Arts
and Crafts Movement, designers interested in the history of
stitching set about examining embroidered fabrics, and even
unpicked old examples from across the world to discover how
they had been worked. New historical texts and instruction
books were written, and the format and names of stitches were
standardised for the first time.

MIRROR, MIRROR
*Shisha stitch, using tiny mirrors,
highlights the traditional chain stitch
design of a contemporary Indian
embroidery in silk rayon.*

INDIAN PATCHWORK
*Fragments of antique fabrics in metallic
threads were salvaged and stitched
together to make this hanging.*

How to Use This Book

The book is divided into six chapters. The first deals with the equipment, threads, and fabrics used for stitchery, and the various techniques involved. This is followed by the Gallery of stitches, which is a visual library of the 234 stitches featured. The stitch instructions are grouped into four chapters – Lines and Borders, Filling Stitches, Openwork, and Needlepoint – each of which has several sub-sections showing the different types of stitches within the group.

GALLERY OF STITCHES

These pages provide a quick visual reference to all the stitches featured in the book. The name of each one is given, followed by the number of the page where the instructions for working it can be found.

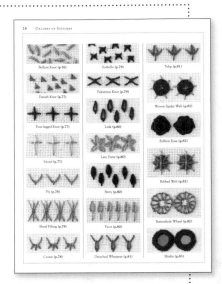

STITCH INSTRUCTION CHAPTERS

STITCH EXAMPLE
Illustrates finished appearance of stitch

OTHER NAME
Shows most common alternatives for stitches with two or more names

LEVEL
Indicates the skill level required to make the stitch – easy, intermediate, or advanced

USES
Suggests practical ways in which each stitch can be used or adapted

METHOD
Describes the way in which the stitch is constructed

MATERIALS
Lists type of fabric, thread, and any other equipment needed

LETTER ANNOTATION
Shows points at which needle enters and exits fabric, in alphabetical order

STITCH VARIATION
Shows another stitch that is worked in a similar way to the main stitch.

TECHNIQUE VARIATION
Illustrates a different way of working the stitch or an alternative colour scheme.

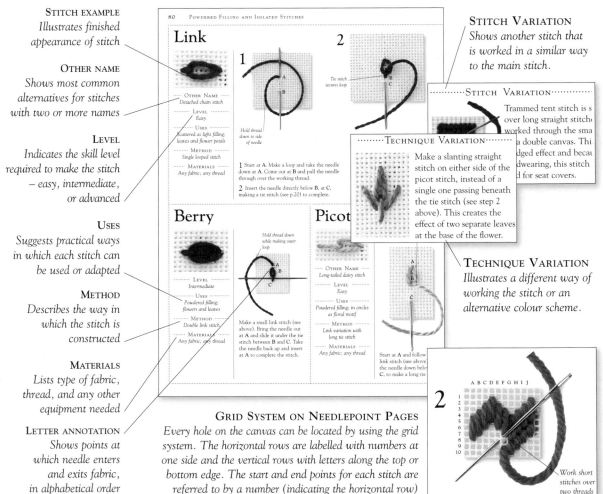

GRID SYSTEM ON NEEDLEPOINT PAGES
Every hole on the canvas can be located by using the grid system. The horizontal rows are labelled with numbers at one side and the vertical rows with letters along the top or bottom edge. The start and end points for each stitch are referred to by a number (indicating the horizontal row) and a letter (indicating the vertical row), eg 9F to 7F.

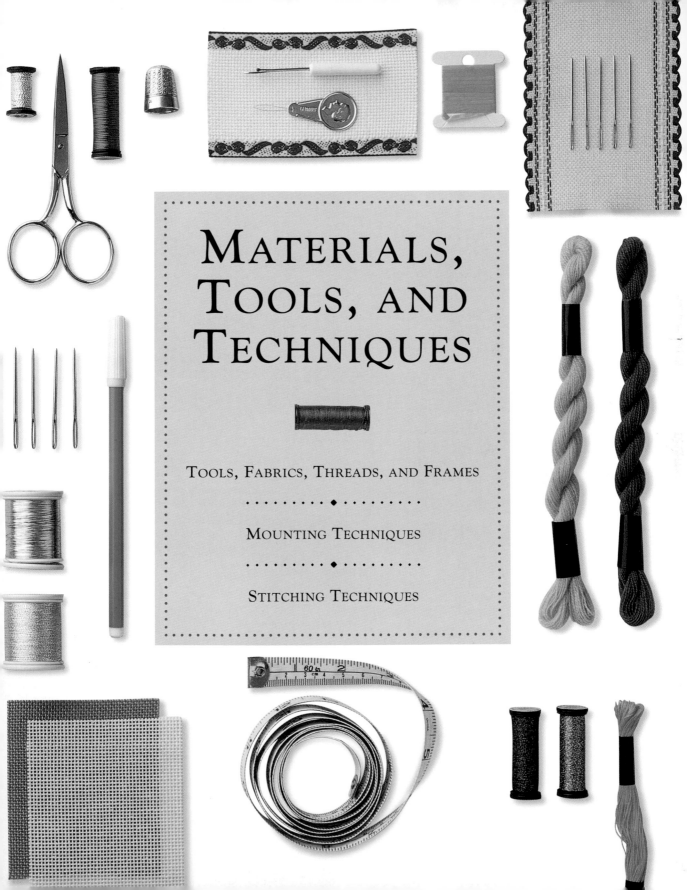

MATERIALS, TOOLS, AND TECHNIQUES

TOOLS, FABRICS, THREADS, AND FRAMES

• • • • • • • ◆ • • • • • • •

MOUNTING TECHNIQUES

• • • • • • • ◆ • • • • • • •

STITCHING TECHNIQUES

Tools, Fabrics, Threads, and Frames

THE BASIC EQUIPMENT required for embroidery is minimal; as with many other sewing crafts, all that is necessary to start stitching is a needle, a length of thread, a piece of cloth, and a pair of scissors. Much time and care will be invested in creating a finished piece of needlework, so the choice of materials at the outset is important. In order to achieve a professional and long-lasting result it is worth investing in the best quality tools, threads, and fabric, and in taking time over their selection.

> ············ HANDY TIP ············
>
> *Purpose-made sewing boxes and fabric-lined wicker baskets are the traditional way, to keep embroidery equipment together in one place. Art storage cases and plastic tool boxes from hardware suppliers provide practical alternatives: they are easy to transport and have many individual compartments in which to store threads, needles, and scissors.*

WORKBOX TOOLS

Every workbox should be equipped with two pairs of sharp, steel-bladed scissors: large shears for cutting out cloth or canvas, and pointed embroidery scissors to clip threads and knots. A stitch ripper is convenient for unpicking mistakes and removing tacking. Dressmaker's pencils or pens are used to draw motifs and guidelines directly on to fabric. Choose a pen with fading ink for any items that cannot be washed, or a watersoluble version for those that will be laundered. Chalk leaves a fine powdered line which can easily be brushed away. A ruler and tape measure may also prove helpful when marking up designs. A needle threader, pins, and thimble are also useful tools.

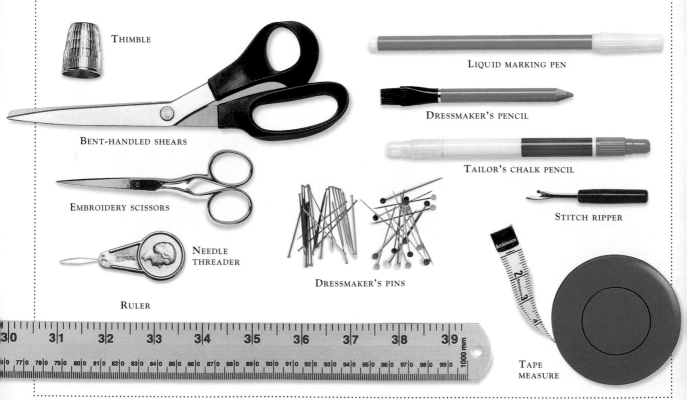

THIMBLE

LIQUID MARKING PEN

DRESSMAKER'S PENCIL

BENT-HANDLED SHEARS

TAILOR'S CHALK PENCIL

EMBROIDERY SCISSORS

STITCH RIPPER

NEEDLE THREADER

DRESSMAKER'S PINS

RULER

TAPE MEASURE

FABRIC AND CANVAS

Stitches can be worked on to any fabric, but there is a wide range designed especially for embroidery. Woven from cotton or linen, the square mesh produces regular, even stitches. They are gauged by the count or number of threads to every 2.5cm (1in): the more threads, the finer the fabric. Use soft, single thread evenweave for counted thread, pulled fabric, and drawn thread work; double thread (Aida, Binca or Hardanger) for geometric patterns and cross stitch; and canvas for needlepoint.

CANVAS
Both single and double weaves come in a variety of weights. Rigid plastic comes in 10-count.

SINGLE CANVAS (INTERLOCK)

SINGLE CANVAS (MONO WEAVE)

PLASTIC CANVAS

DOUBLE CANVAS

EVENWEAVE FABRIC
Manufactured in gauges from 8- to 36-count, this is available in many colours and textures.

SINGLE THREAD EVENWEAVE

HARDANGER FABRIC

BINCA

AIDA CLOTH

PLAINWEAVE FABRIC
Decorative silk, felt, cotton stripes, and checks are all ideal for freestyle stitching.

LINEN

FELT

SILK TAFFETA

STRIPED TICKING

COTTON GINGHAM

WOVEN BANDS
Narrow strips of fabric with decorative woven edges such as this natural linen band, are available in various widths.

THREADS

Embroidery threads come in myriad colours and a broad spectrum of textures and weights. The thickness of the thread dictates the size and shape of the stitch, which will have a very different appearance if worked in a fine matt yarn or a lustrous pearl cotton. Certain wools and threads are spun in a single strand, whilst others consist of up to six fine strands which are loosely twisted together. These can be separated out and re-combined, depending on the effect or line width required. The needle can be threaded with strands of two or more colours to create subtle shaded effects. Manufacturer's sample books and shade cards show the full range of different threads that are available and can be a good source of inspiration when planning a new project.

SILKS AND COTTONS

Silks and cottons are made in both single and stranded skeins. Silk, rayon, and twisted pearl cotton all have a high sheen, whilst stranded cotton gives a smooth finish. Use fine flower thread or the thicker soft cotton for a more matt appearance. Metallic threads add textural interest, and silk ribbon is used for embroidering naturalistic roses and flowers.

FLOWER THREAD

STRANDED COTTON

SILK RIBBON   METALLIC THREAD

SOFT COTTON

SILK THREAD   SILK THREAD

CREWEL WOOL

SILK RAYON

STRANDED SILK

PEARL COTTON

WOOLS

The thickest wool is 4-ply tapestry, used on 10- to 14-count canvas. Use several strands of fine 2-ply crewel on canvas or a single strand on fabric. Persian has three easily separated medium-weight strands: use two or three for needlepoint and one to stitch on fabric.

TAPESTRY WOOL

PERSIAN WOOL

NEEDLES

The correct choice of needle is essential for any piece of embroidery or needlepoint. There are five different types used for decorative stitching, each with a particular purpose. All come in a range of thicknesses and lengths; select one that can be threaded easily and that passes smoothly through the fabric without snagging the thread.

Types of Needle

Chenille needles have sharp points, designed for working on heavy plainweave fabrics with thick threads. Blunt tapestry needles with long oval eyes are used with evenweave fabric and canvas, interlacing, and for all pulled fabric and drawn thread work. Versatile crewel needles are used for most embroidery stitches. They are long with easily-threaded eyes which take one or more strands. Sharps are mainly used for hand-sewing but, like betweens, they are ideal for fine stitching and French knots.

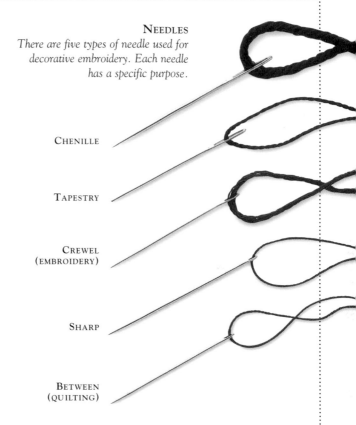

NEEDLES
There are five types of needle used for decorative embroidery. Each needle has a specific purpose.

CHENILLE

TAPESTRY

CREWEL
(EMBROIDERY)

SHARP

BETWEEN
(QUILTING)

PREPARING THE THREAD

A length of thread can be easily unwound from a reel, but care must be taken when working with cotton or wools that come in individual skeins. Twisted skeins have to be undone before they can be used, but the paper bands should not be removed from looped skeins or they will become tangled. To prevent the thread becoming damaged as it passes repeatedly through the fabric, cut off a working length of no more than 50cm (20in). Use a needle threader with fine cotton and silk or the loop method of threading (see below) for stranded and pearl threads or wool.

Keep slip knot loose

UNTYING A TWISTED SKEIN
Remove the paper bands. Untwist the skein and cut through the threads, then tie them together with a loose slip knot.

Pull thread out gently

USING A LOOPED SKEIN
Leave the bands in place. Hold one end of the skein firmly and draw out the loose thread to the required length.

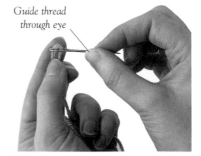

Guide thread through eye

THREADING A NEEDLE
Fold thread over needle and hold the loop between thumb and finger. Slide the loop off; pass it through the eye.

FRAMES

Small-scale projects and some needlepoint can be stitched in the hand, but most embroidery has to be worked on a frame to achieve the best result. The frame maintains the fabric at an even tension and holds the grain straight, which keeps the stitches regular and even, and protects the work by reducing the amount of handling it undergoes. The choice of frame depends on both the scale of a project and the fabric being used, but is very often a personal preference. There are three basic types: fixed stretchers and adjustable scroll frames which are used for embroidery fabrics and all weights of canvas, and round hoops for cotton and linen. All of these are available with integral or additional stand attachments, which give the advantage of freeing up both hands for stitching. Larger embroideries in particular are manageable if worked on a free-standing frame. Any frame should be large enough to accommodate the whole design area; moving fabric within a frame can damage the stitches.

SQUARE AND RECTANGULAR FRAMES

These can be used for canvas or embroidery fabric. Stretcher frames are sold as two pairs of struts which can be chosen and assembled to fit a particular piece of work. Scroll frames come in several widths, depending on the roller length.

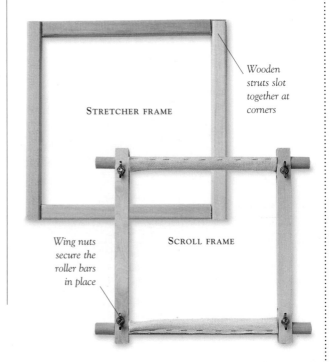

STRETCHER FRAME

Wooden struts slot together at corners

Wing nuts secure the roller bars in place

SCROLL FRAME

ROUND FRAMES

Wooden hoop frames range in diameter from 12 to 32cm (4⅘ to 13in) and are ideal for smaller pieces of embroidery worked on fabric. They are light, portable, and easily held in one hand, but free-standing versions, which can be clamped on to a table, are also available.

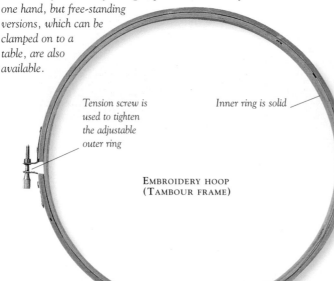

Tension screw is used to tighten the adjustable outer ring

Inner ring is solid

EMBROIDERY HOOP
(TAMBOUR FRAME)

PREPARING THE INNER RING

To prevent delicate fabrics from becoming damaged and to stop them slipping within the hoop, bind the inner ring tightly with narrow cotton tape or bias binding. Stitch the two ends together to secure.

Mounting Techniques

IT IS WORTH taking time at the outset of a project to prepare and mount the fabric properly. Neaten the edges to prevent them fraying or snagging by working a narrow hem or a machine zigzag stitch around linen and cotton fabrics, or by binding canvas with masking tape. Use a steam iron to press the fabric and remove any creases.

.... HANDY TIP ....
Before mounting the fabric, fold it into quarters and work two rows of tacking along the creases, following the weave. Keep these lines straight to ensure that the grain of the fabric does not become distorted when stretched in the frame.

USING AN EMBROIDERY HOOP
The fabric should be at least 8cm (3in) larger all round than the diameter of the hoop. Loosen the screw slightly before mounting.

MOUNTING THE FABRIC
Centre the fabric over the inner ring, then gently push the outer ring over the fabric, keeping the grain straight. Tighten the screw to hold the frame together.

PREPARING A STRETCHER FRAME
The neatened fabric or canvas should be the same size as the frame. Use drawing pins or a staple gun to fix the fabric in place.

PINNING CANVAS
Mark the middle of each strut; line the canvas up to these four points. Pin from the centre out towards each corner, spacing the pins at regular intervals.

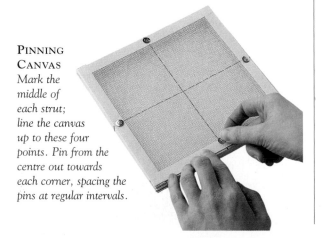

SETTING UP A SCROLL FRAME
Cut the fabric or canvas to the same width as the webbing. If it is longer than the struts, any surplus can be wrapped round the bottom roller and adjusted as work progresses.

1 *Neaten the side edges. Match the midpoints of the canvas and webbing, then tack together. Sewing outwards from the centre, work herringbone stitch (see p.52) over the join.*

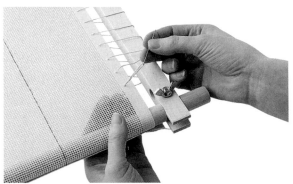

2 *Slot the rollers into the spaces in the struts. Tighten the two top screws, then turn the bottom roller to stretch the fabric. Secure the other screws, then lace the fabric tightly over the edges using thin string and a tapestry needle.*

Stitching Techniques

THE KEY TO a professional finish for any piece of
needlework is to keep the length of the stitches
regular and to maintain even tension throughout, whether
or not the fabric is mounted on a frame. Take time to sew
a small sample piece before embarking on any new
project, to become familiar with the stitches and to
establish a rhythmic pattern of working. Embroidery
stitches are constructed either vertically, usually from top
to bottom, or horizontally towards the left or right,
although they may appear at any angle in the finished
piece. Needlepoint fillings, which form all-over patterns,
are worked in diagonal, horizontal, or vertical rows.

> ··· LEFT-HANDED WORKERS ···
>
> *All the illustrations in the following
> chapters show how the stitches would
> be sewn by a right-handed worker, but
> most left-handed stitchers will prefer to
> sew in the opposite direction. Hold a
> small mirror in front of the page to
> turn the step-by-step diagrams the
> other way round and to reverse the
> direction of the needle.*

BEGINNING TO STITCH
Follow one of the two techniques shown below
to start off or to join a new length of thread.
Both will help to ensure that the reverse side
of the stitching is as neat as the front.

FASTENING OFF A THREAD
Fasten off the thread when it is no less than
10cm (4in) long. Try not to finish too many
threads in the same area as this can create an
uneven surface, especially in needlepoint.

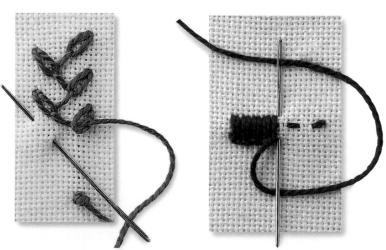

LOST KNOT METHOD
*Use this technique for needlepoint and
open embroidery stitches. Knot one end
of the thread and insert the needle from
the front, a short distance along the
line to be worked. Continue stitching
so the thread is held down at the back
by the first stitches. Cut off the knot.*

RUNNING STITCH METHOD
*Use when working embroidery stitches
which are spaced closely together and
for needlepoint. Leaving a loose end of
thread at the back, work a few small
running stitches, and stitch over them.
The end can then be darned through
the reverse of the stitches.*

FASTENING OFF
*Take the needle through to the wrong
side of the fabric and turn the work
over. Pass the needle under the loops at
the back of the final few stitches for a
distance of about 2.5cm (1in), then
clip the end of the thread close to the
fabric surface.*

WAYS OF WORKING
Holding the fabric in the hand is a familiar sewing technique and some stitches, including looped embroidery stitches, are best worked this way. When the fabric is mounted in a frame, a special two-handed technique is used.

Embroidering in the Hand
Support the area being worked over the fore-finger. Hold the needle in the other hand and slide it in and out in a single movement.

LOOPED STITCHES
Loop the thread from one side to the other and use the free thumb to hold it down. Pull the needle through over the working thread. The step-by-step diagrams will indicate the point where the thread should be held.

Using Both Hands
Working with a free-standing frame may prove awkward at first but, with practice, both right- and left-handed workers will find that they can stitch quickly and evenly with two hands.

STABBING TECHNIQUE
Keep one hand on either side of the frame. Push the needle down into the fabric from the top and pull it through from below. Pass it back up with this hand, and draw it through from above.

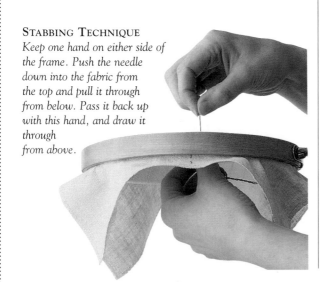

Hand-held Needlepoint
Straight, and some crossed, stitches can be worked in the hand without any problems, but diagonal stitches will cause some distortion.

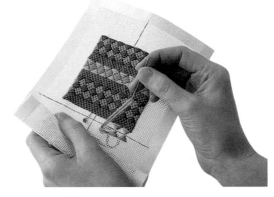

STITCHING ON CANVAS
Bind the edges of the canvas and start at the far side. Keep the unworked part rolled in one hand, while stitching with the other. Be sure to keep the tension even.

WORKING NEEDLEPOINT STITCHES
Stitches on canvas are worked into the square holes between the woven threads. To avoid splitting the stitches, always try to bring the needle up through an unworked space and take it down into an already worked hole. Do not pull the yarn too tightly or the holes will become enlarged so the canvas shows through.

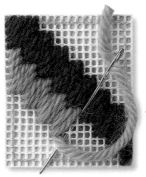 

1 *Work the first row, then fill in the bottom corner. Start each stitch from an unworked hole and insert the needle in to the base of the stitches in the previous row.*

2 *Fill the top corner with stitches worked in the opposite direction, ending each one at the top of the last row. Use this method with the stabbing technique.*

WORKING FILLING STITCHES

Powdered, open, and solid fillings, along with most needlepoint stitches, are worked within a specific area of a design, which may be a naturalistic leaf or petal, or a more regular geometric form. The size and shape of the individual stitches have to be altered to fill the given shape. For open and solid embroidered fillings, this means that the stitches must be worked at different lengths to fit within a curved or zigzag line, or all at the same length to complete a rectangular or square motif. Powdered fillings are worked singly within an outline: their size may be varied to add extra visual interest. Diagonal needlepoint stitches, which have a regular, all-over surface pattern, require part stitches to be worked at the edges of the shape.

OPEN AND SOLID FILLINGS
Start a leaf at the top with a short straight stitch to fill in the point, then work downwards, first increasing, then reducing the length of the stitches. Insert the needle just beyond the edge of the shape so the stitches hide the line.

POWDERED FILLINGS
Work a fine outline stitch over the guideline to define the motif, then fill the shape with individual stitches. These can be arranged in a regular pattern or scattered randomly within the leaf.

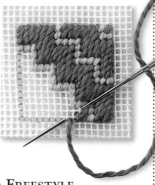

NEEDLEPOINT FILLINGS
Straight, cross, and star stitches fit easily within a square, but diagonal stitches have to be adapted. Count the intersections carefully, and make part stitches to square off the edges of the area being worked.

COUNTED THREAD AND FREESTYLE

Embroidery stitches can be worked on either evenweave or plainweave fabric. A regularly spaced effect can easily be created by counting the threads on evenweave; work between guidelines to achieve the same result with freestyle stitching on finer plainweave fabric.

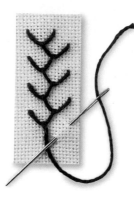

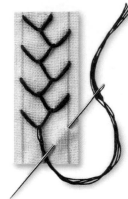

EVENWEAVE FABRIC
Make each stitch over the same number of threads or thread intersections.

PLAINWEAVE FABRIC
Stitch between two parallel lines drawn on to the fabric with a dressmaker's pen.

TIE STITCHES

These short stitches are used to anchor looped stitches such as chain stitch, in couching, and to bunch together groups of straight stitches.

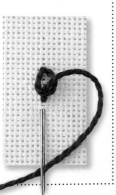

MAKING A TIE STITCH
Bring the needle up above the long stitch or inside the loop and insert it just below the thread.

WORKING OPENWORK STITCHES

In all types of openwork the background fabric is as important as the stitches themselves, and forms an integral part of the finished piece. It has to be carefully prepared for drawn thread work and for insertion (faggoting) stitches.

Drawn Thread Stitches

The open spaces that give drawn thread work its characteristic lacy appearance are formed by removing some of the woven threads that make up the fabric.

PULLING OUT THE THREADS
Evenweave cotton or linen are the best fabrics to work with. Use the point of a needle to lift up the threads and pull out enough to make an open band or bands of the required width.

Insertion Stitches

To ensure that the space between the two hems remains constant and the stitches are worked regularly, the fabric being joined has to be stitched on to paper before starting.

MOUNTING THE FABRIC
Stitch a narrow hem along each long edge. Draw two parallel lines, 6mm (¼in) apart on to a strip of heavy paper. With the right sides facing, tack one piece of fabric along each line.

FINISHING OFF

When the final stitches have been completed, take the work off the frame. Press embroidery lightly on the wrong side before mounting.

Blocking

A piece of needlepoint which incorporates diagonal stitches will inevitably become pulled out of shape as it is worked. Any distortion can be remedied by blocking the canvas.

HOW TO BLOCK
Make a template of the finished piece and mark into quarters. Tape to a board and cover with polythene. Place the dampened work face down. Match the centre top edge to the template and pin. Stretch and pin the bottom edge and two sides. Insert more pins at 2.5cm (1in) intervals. Allow to dry.

Mounting

If a project is to be framed it should first be mounted on to board to keep it in shape, whether it is worked on fabric or canvas.

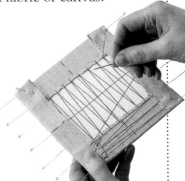

1 *Cut the board to size and mark into quarters. Centre it on the wrong side of the fabric and fold back long edges. Pin them to the card from the centre out.*

2 *Using strong thread, lace the edges together. Do the same with the other two sides. Check the fabric is centred, then tighten up and secure the threads.*

GALLERY
OF
STITCHES

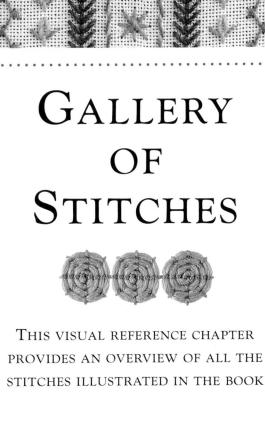

THIS VISUAL REFERENCE CHAPTER
PROVIDES AN OVERVIEW OF ALL THE
STITCHES ILLUSTRATED IN THE BOOK

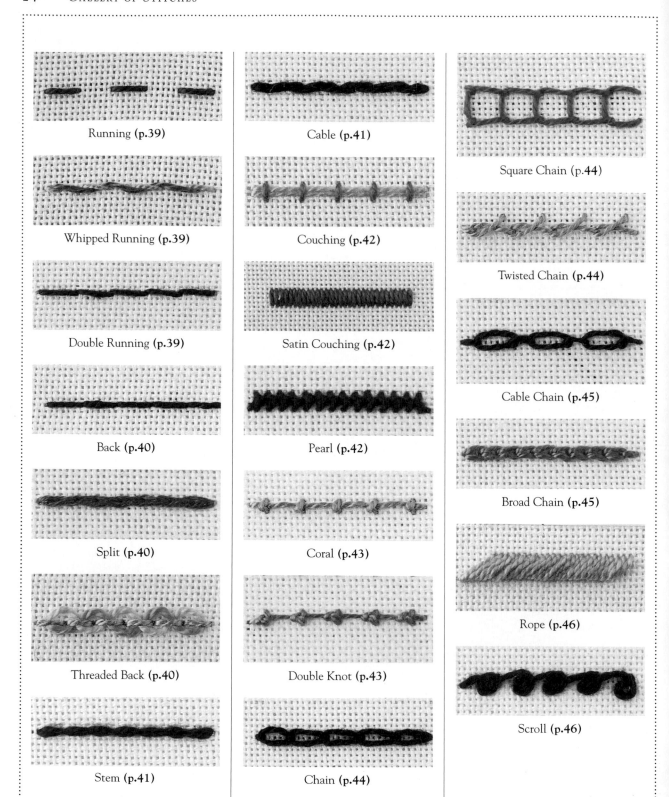

Running **(p.39)**

Cable **(p.41)**

Square Chain (p.44)

Whipped Running **(p.39)**

Couching **(p.42)**

Twisted Chain **(p.44)**

Double Running **(p.39)**

Satin Couching **(p.42)**

Cable Chain **(p.45)**

Back **(p.40)**

Pearl **(p.42)**

Broad Chain **(p.45)**

Split **(p.40)**

Coral **(p.43)**

Rope **(p.46)**

Threaded Back **(p.40)**

Double Knot **(p.43)**

Scroll **(p.46)**

Stem **(p.41)**

Chain **(p.44)**

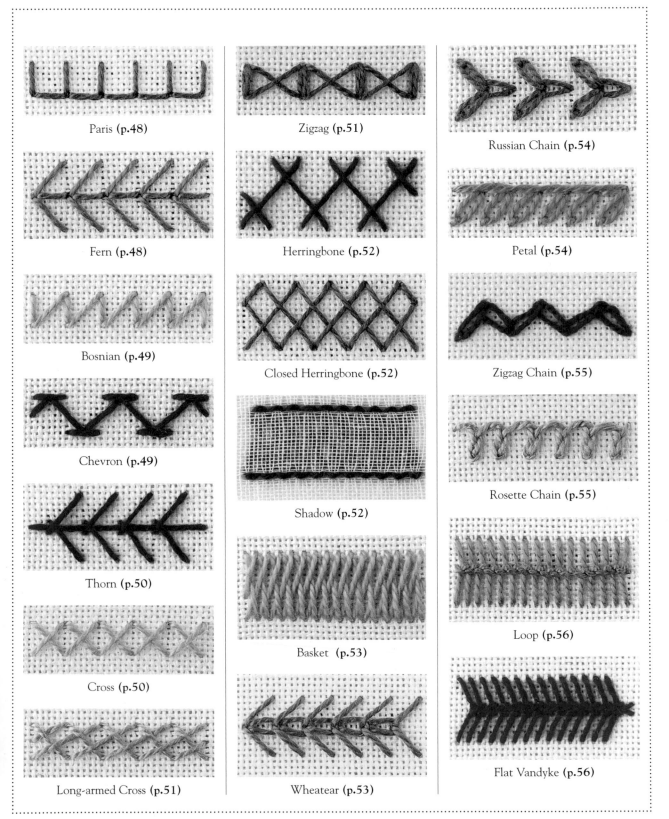

Paris (p.48)

Zigzag (p.51)

Russian Chain (p.54)

Fern (p.48)

Herringbone (p.52)

Petal (p.54)

Bosnian (p.49)

Closed Herringbone (p.52)

Zigzag Chain (p.55)

Chevron (p.49)

Shadow (p.52)

Rosette Chain (p.55)

Thorn (p.50)

Basket (p.53)

Loop (p.56)

Cross (p.50)

Long-armed Cross (p.51)

Wheatear (p.53)

Flat Vandyke (p.56)

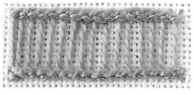

Ladder (p.57)

Blanket (p.58)

Buttonhole (p.58)

Closed Buttonhole (p.58)

Single Feather (p.58)

Up and Down Buttonhole (p.59)

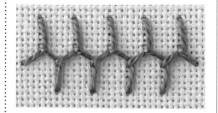

Open Cretan (p.59)

Feather (p.60)

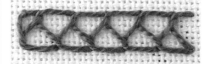

Closed Feather (p.60)

Double Feather (p.61)

Chained Feather (p.61)

Pekinese (p.63)

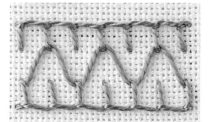

Laced Buttonhole (p.63)

Interlacing Band (p.63)

Magic Chain (p.64)

Singalese Chain (p.64)

Threaded Chain (p.65)

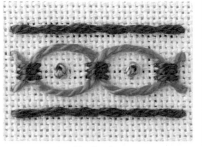

Guilloche (p.65)

Raised Chevron (p.66)

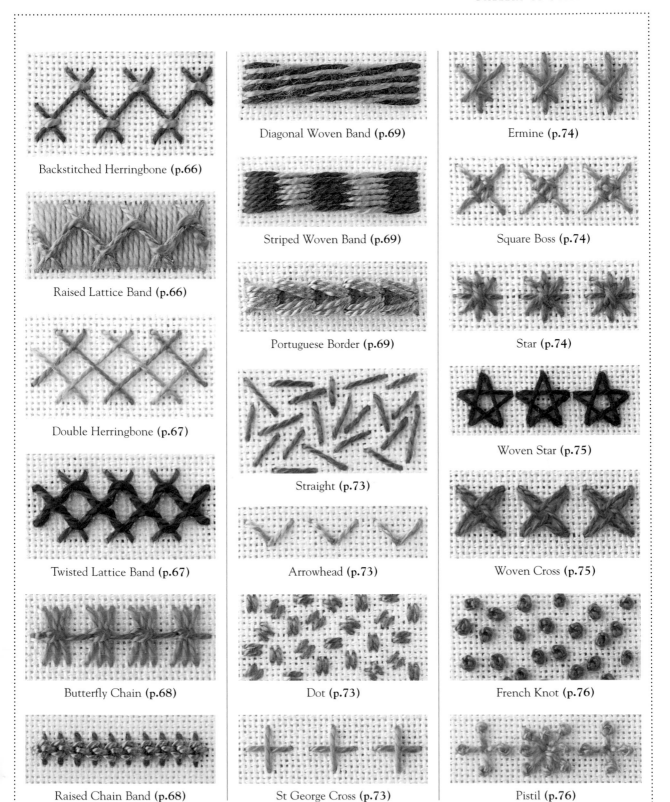

Backstitched Herringbone (p.66)

Raised Lattice Band (p.66)

Double Herringbone (p.67)

Twisted Lattice Band (p.67)

Butterfly Chain (p.68)

Raised Chain Band (p.68)

Diagonal Woven Band (p.69)

Striped Woven Band (p.69)

Portuguese Border (p.69)

Straight (p.73)

Arrowhead (p.73)

Dot (p.73)

St George Cross (p.73)

Ermine (p.74)

Square Boss (p.74)

Star (p.74)

Woven Star (p.75)

Woven Cross (p.75)

French Knot (p.76)

Pistil (p.76)

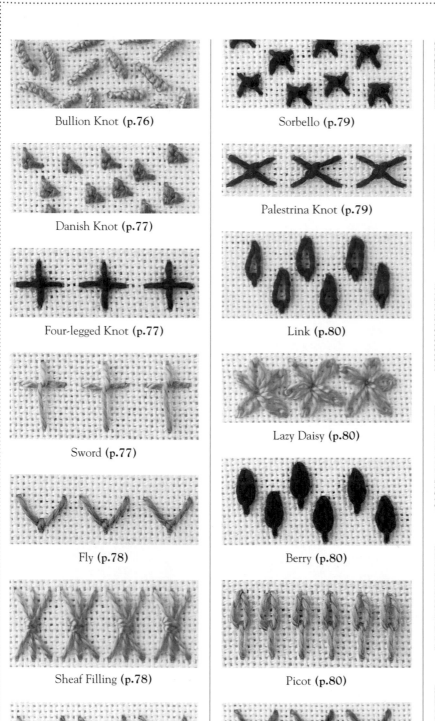

Bullion Knot (p.76)

Danish Knot (p.77)

Four-legged Knot (p.77)

Sword (p.77)

Fly (p.78)

Sheaf Filling (p.78)

Crown (p.78)

Sorbello (p.79)

Palestrina Knot (p.79)

Link (p.80)

Lazy Daisy (p.80)

Berry (p.80)

Picot (p.80)

Detached Wheatear (p.81)

Tulip (p.81)

Woven Spider Web (p.82)

Ribbon Rose (p.82)

Ribbed Web (p.82)

Buttonhole Wheel (p.82)

Shisha (p.83)

Darning (**p.85**)

Double Darning (**p.85**)

Brick and Cross (**p.85**)

Satin (**p.86**)

Surface Satin (**p.86**)

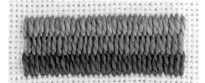

Encroaching Satin (**p.86**)

Long and Short (**p.87**)

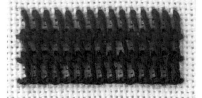

Buttonhole Filling (**p.87**)

Stem Filling (**p.87**)

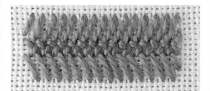

Leaf (**p.88**)

Open Fishbone (**p.88**)

Attached Fly (**p.89**)

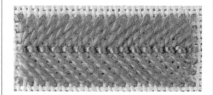

Close Fly (**p.89**)

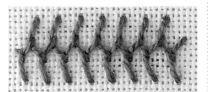

Cretan (**p.89**)

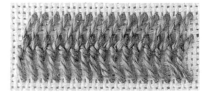

Close Cretan (**p.89**)

Romanian Couching (**p.90**)

Bokhara Couching (**p.90**)

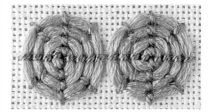

Spiral Couching (**p.90**)

Couched Filling (**p.91**)

Laidwork **(p.91)**

Back Stitch Trellis **(p.92)**

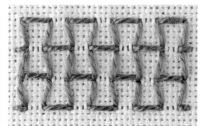

Japanese Darning **(p.92)**

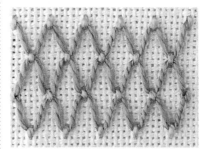

Cloud Filling **(p.93)**

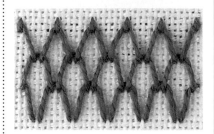

Wave Filling **(p.93)**

Window Filling **(p.97)**

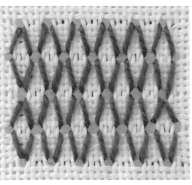

Pulled Wave Filling **(p.97)**

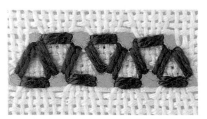

Three-sided **(p.97)**

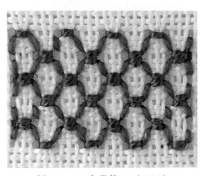

Honeycomb Filling **(p.98)**

Russian Filling **(p.98)**

Diagonal Raised Band **(p.99)**

Ridged Filling **(p.99)**

Punch **(p.99)**

Cobbler Filling **(p.100)**

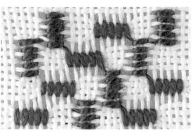

Step (**p.100**)

Mosaic Filling (**p.101**)

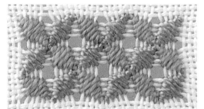

Diagonal Satin Filling (**p.101**)

Back Stitch Rings (**p.102**)

Algerian Eye (**p.102**)

Outlined Diamond Eyelet (**p.103**)

Single Hem (**p.105**)

Ladder Hem (**p.105**)

Serpentine Hem (**p.105**)

Antique Hem (**p.105**)

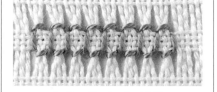

Italian Border (**p.106**)

Four-sided (**p.106**)

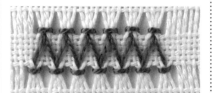

Chevron Border (**p.107**)

Diamond Border (**p.107**)

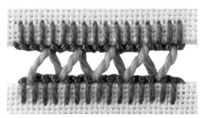

Laced Insertion (**p.108**)

Faggot Bundles (**p.108**)

Cretan Insertion (**p.108**)

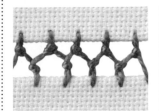

Knotted Insertion (p.109)

Buttonhole Insertion
(p.109)

Needleweaving Bars
(p.110)

Zigzag Clusters (p.110)

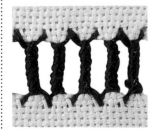

Corded Clusters (p.110)

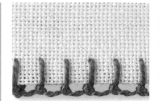

Antwerp Edging (p.112)

Sailor Edging (p.112)

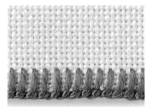

Looped Edge (p.113)

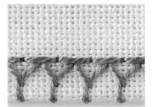

Half Chevron (p.113)

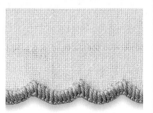

Scalloped Edge
(p.114)

Ring Picot Edge (p.114)

Buttonhole Eyelet
(p.115)

Overcast Eyelet (p.115)

Square Eyelet (p.115)

Upright Gobelin (p.119)

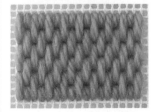

Gobelin Filling (p.119)

Parisian (p.119)

Hungarian (p.120)

Hungarian Diamond
(p.120)

Single Twill (p.121)

Double Twill (p.121)

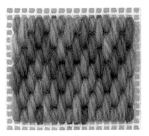

Bargello (p.121)

Chevron (p.122)

Hungarian Ground (p.122)

Straight Cushion (p.123)

Scottish Diamond (p.123)

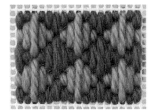

Diamond (p.124)

Long Stitch Triangles (p.124)

Lozenge (p.125)

Straight Milanese (p.125)

Double Brick (p.126)

Brick Filling (p.126)

Long and Short Brick (p.127)

Basket Filling (p.127)

Half Cross (p.129)

Basketweave Tent (p.129)

Tent (p.129)

Trammed Tent (p.129)

Gobelin (p.130)

Encroaching Gobelin (p.130)

Reversed Sloping Gobelin (p.131)

Canvas Stem (p.131)

Florence (p.132)

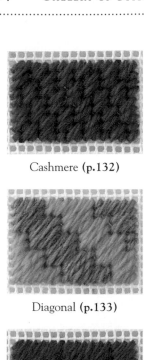

Cashmere **(p.132)**

Diagonal **(p.133)**

Byzantine **(p.133)**

Jacquard **(p.134)**

Milanese **(p.135)**

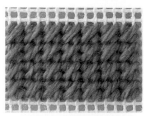

Mosaic **(p.136)**

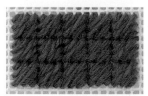

Cushion **(p.136)**

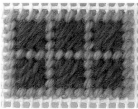

Scottish **(p.137)**

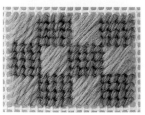

Chequer **(p.137)**

Moorish **(p.135)**

Cross **(p.139)**

Diagonal Cross **(p.139)**

Double Cross **(p.139)**

Upright Cross **(p.140)**

Diamond Cross **(p.140)**

Smyrna Cross **(p.140)**

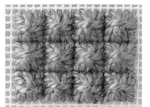

Double Leviathan **(p.141)**

Diagonal Tweed **(p.141)**

Broad Cross **(p.142)**

Cross-corner Cushion **(p.142)**

Brighton **(p.143)**

Rice (**p.143**)

Plaited Gobelin (**p.144**)

Greek (**p.144**)

Plait (**p.145**)

Fishbone (**p.145**)

Fern (**p.146**)

Fir (**p.146**)

Rhodes (**p.147**)

Half Rhodes (**p.147**)

Star (**p.148**)

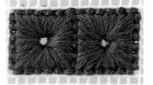

Eye (**p.148**)

Diamond Eye (**p.149**)

Fan (**p.149**)

Rya (**p.151**)

Turkey (**p.151**)

Houndstooth (**p.152**)

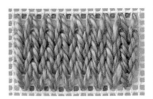

Knitting (**p.153**)

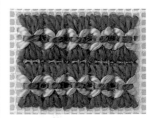

Old Wheatsheaf (**p.153**)

Tied Gobelin (**p.154**)

French (**p.154**)

Pineapple (**p.155**)

Arrow (**p.155**)

LINE AND BORDER STITCHES

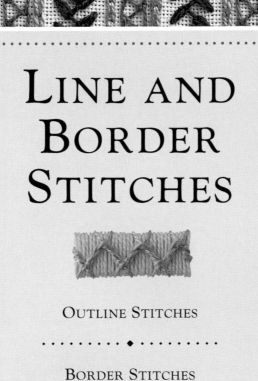

OUTLINE STITCHES

· · · · · · ◆ · · · · · ·

BORDER STITCHES

· · · · · · ◆ · · · · · ·

COMPOSITE BORDER STITCHES

Outline Stitches

THIS GROUP INCLUDES some of the most basic and versatile embroidery stitches, which are all worked continuously in a curved or straight row. They can be sewn in any thread on any fabric, depending on the effect required, and are employed whenever fine lines and details are needed. Use these stitches to 'draw' designs and motifs, for monograms and lettering, or to define shapes which will be completed with filling stitches. Running and back stitches provide the foundation for some composite stitches and can be interlaced with contrasting threads.

Running

········ LEVEL ········
Easy

········· USES ·········
*Simple lines and outlines;
basis for other stitches;
hand sewing and quilting;
reinforcement for cutwork*

······· METHOD ·······
*Regularly spaced straight
stitches of equal length*

······ MATERIALS ······
Any fabric; any thread

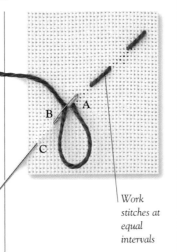

Work stitches at equal intervals

Come up at **A**, then insert the needle at **B**. Bring it out again at **C**. Continue, spacing the stitches evenly and making them all the same length.

Whipped Running

····· OTHER NAME ·····
Cordonnet stitch

········ LEVEL ········
Easy

········· USES ·········
Straight or curved outlines

······· METHOD ·······
Laced running stitch

······ MATERIALS ······
*Any fabric; any two
threads – contrasting
colours and thicknesses for
greater effect; blunt needle
for whipping*

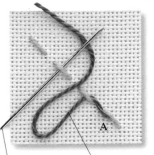

Use blunt needle to avoid catching threads   *Do not pull lacing thread tightly*

Work a foundation of closely spaced running stitch (see left). Using a blunt needle, bring the second thread up at **A**. Slide the needle under the next stitch from right to left and pull through gently. Continue whipping to the end of the line.

Double Running

········· 1 ·········

Ensure spaces are equal in length to stitches

Make stitches all same length

····· OTHER NAMES ·····
*Holbein stitch;
Assisi stitch*

········· LEVEL ·········
Easy

········· USES ·········
*With cross stitch; in Assisi
and blackwork*

······· METHOD ·······
*Counted thread stitch
worked with two rows of
running stitch*

······ MATERIALS ······
*Evenweave fabric; any
embroidery thread*

········· 2 ·········

Angle needle to ensure a smooth line

1 Work a line of running stitch (see above). Make sure the stitches are all the same length and equal in length to the spaces.

2 Fill in the spaces on the return journey. Come out at the top of the previous stitch, at **A**. Insert the needle just below the start of the next stitch at **B**. Repeat to the end of the row.

···TECHNIQUE VARIATION···

Double running stitch can be used to create intricate geometric bands and filling patterns. Chart the design on squared paper. Stitch along the line, working every other stitch. On the return journey, fill in the spaces with a second row of running stitch worked in the opposite direction.

Back

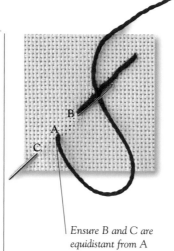

········· LEVEL ·········
Easy

········· USES ·········
Details and fine outlines, lettering, basis for other composite stitches

······ MATERIALS ······
Any fabric; any thread – untwisted threads give smooth effect

Ensure B and C are equidistant from A

Come up at **A**. Insert the needle at **B**, then bring it out again one stitch length ahead of **A** at **C**. Insert the needle again at **A** and continue making regular backward stitches in the same way.

Split

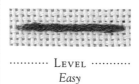

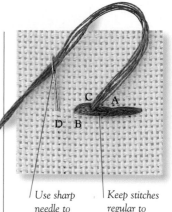

········· LEVEL ·········
Easy

········· USES ·········
Outlines; in close rows as filling; padded edge for solid filling stitches

······ MATERIALS ······
Any fabric; soft, untwisted thread such as stranded cotton or silk floss; sharp needle

Use sharp needle to divide thread easily

Keep stitches regular to create smooth surface

Come up at **A** and work a straight stitch across to **B**. Bring the needle up at **C**, half-way along the stitch, so that it splits the thread. Pull through. Insert the needle at **D** and repeat to continue.

Threaded Back

········· LEVEL ··········
Easy

·········· USES ··········
Flexible, decorative outlines and borders

········ METHOD ·········
Row of back stitch interlaced with one or two threads

······· MATERIALS ·······
Any fabric; two or three colours of any thick embroidery thread; blunt needle

1

Do not pull thread too tightly

Use blunt needle to avoid catching threads

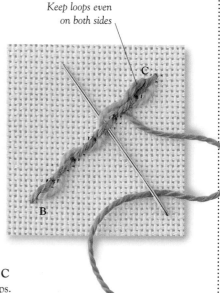

2

Keep loops even on both sides

1 Work a foundation of back stitch (see above). Bring the second thread up at **A**. Slide the needle under the next stitch, then pass it back under the following stitch. Continue weaving from side to side.

2 Take the thread down at **B** and finish off. For a double-threaded variation bring another thread up at **C** and weave in the same way as before, filling in the gaps.

Stem

····· OTHER NAMES ·····
Outline stitch;
crewel stitch

·········· LEVEL ··········
Easy

············ USES ············
Outlines; flower stems;
worked in rows as filling

······· MATERIALS ·······
Any fabric;
any embroidery thread
or crewel wool

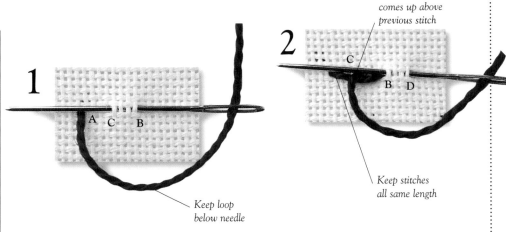

Ensure thread
comes up above
previous stitch

Keep loop
below needle

Keep stitches
all same length

1 Start at **A**, then insert the needle at **B**. Bring the needle up in the centre at **C**.

2 Insert the needle at **D** and bring it out at the end of the previous stitch, at **B**. Continue making a row of overlapping stitches.

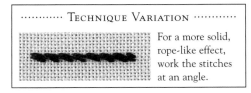

··········· TECHNIQUE VARIATION ···········

For a more solid, rope-like effect, work the stitches at an angle.

Cable

····· OTHER NAMES ·····
Alternating stem stitch;
side-to-side stem stitch

·········· LEVEL ··········
Easy

············ USES ············
Straight and curved
outlines; narrow border

······· MATERIALS ·······
Any fabric;
any embroidery thread

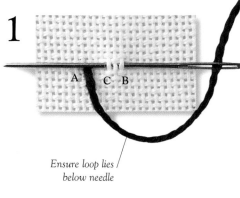

Ensure loop lies
below needle

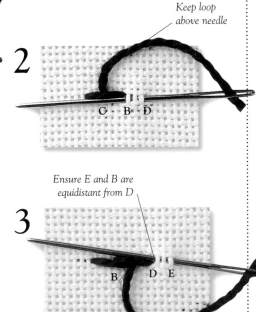

Keep loop
above needle

Ensure E and B are
equidistant from D

1 Start at **A**, then insert the needle at **B**. Bring the needle up in the centre at **C** and pull through.

2 Insert the needle at **D** and bring it back up at **B**.

3 Keeping the loop below the needle, insert at **E** and come up again at **D**. Repeat steps 2 and 3 to continue stitching.

Couching

.... LEVEL ....
Easy

.... USES ....
Straight and curved outlines; metal thread work; in rows as filling

.... METHOD ....
Laid threads held down with small tie stitches

.... MATERIALS ....
Any closely woven fabric; thick or delicate embroidery threads; finer thread for couching; frame

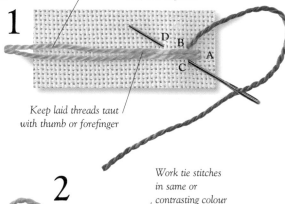

Vary number of laid threads depending on thickness of line required

1

Keep laid threads taut with thumb or forefinger

2

Work tie stitches in same or contrasting colour

1 Bring the main threads out at **A** and lay them along the line to be worked. To make the tie stitches (see p.20), come up at **B** using the couching thread. Insert the needle at **C**, over the laid threads, and bring it out at **D** to start the next stitch.

2 Continue working evenly spaced tie stitches over the laid thread to the end of the line. Finish off all threads at the back.

.... STITCH VARIATION ....

Satin couching, known also as trailing stitch, is a variation of couching, in which the tie stitches are worked very closely together so that the laid thread is completely covered.

Pearl

.... LEVEL ....
Intermediate

.... USES ....
Intricate or straight outlines; monograms

.... METHOD ....
Knotted stitch, worked in continuous line

.... MATERIALS ....
Any fabric; thick, non-stranded embroidery thread

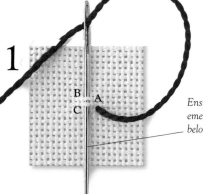

1

Ensure needle emerges directly below B

2

Do not pull stitch too tightly

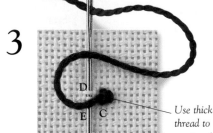

3

Use thick thread to create raised knot

1 Start at **A** and make a diagonal stitch up to **B**. Bring the needle out at **C**.

2 Pull the thread to form a loop. Slide the needle under the stitch from right to left.

3 Tighten the knot by pulling the thread gently downwards. Take the needle up to the left and insert at **D** to form the loop for the next stitch. Come out at **E**. Repeat steps 2 and 3 to continue along the row.

Coral

····· OTHER NAMES ·····
*Knotted stitch; snail trail;
beaded stitch*

·········· LEVEL ··········
Easy

·········· USES ··········
*Straight and curved
outlines; in rows as
textured filling*

········· METHOD ·········
*Series of closely or widely
spaced single knots*

····· MATERIALS ······
*Any fabric; thick,
non-stranded thread*

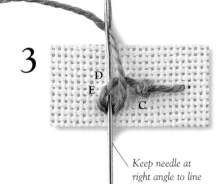

1
B   A
C
*Hold down thread with
thumb or forefinger*

*Ensure thread
loop lies under
needle*

2
C

3
D
E   C

*Keep needle at
right angle to line*

1 Start at **A** and hold the thread down along the stitching line. Insert the needle at **B** and loop the thread from left to right. Bring the point out over the loop at **C**.

2 Pull the needle gently through the loop so that the thread tightens into a knot.

3 Take the needle across to the left and insert it at **D**. Bring it out at **E**, ready for the next knot. Repeat steps 1 and 2 to continue.

Double Knot

····· OTHER NAMES ·····
*Old English knot stitch;
Palestrina stitch;
Smyrna stitch*

·········· LEVEL ··········
Intermediate

········· METHOD ·········
*Knotted stitch, worked in
continuous line*

·········· USES ··········
Outlines and borders

····· MATERIALS ······
*Any fabric; thick,
non-stranded
embroidery thread*

1
A   B
C

*Avoid catching thread
or fabric with needle*

2
C

*Pass needle over
looped thread*

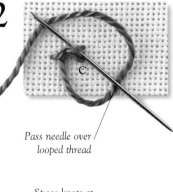

*Space knots at
regular intervals: for
more texture, place
closer together*

3
C   D
E

1 Start at **A** and make a diagonal stitch across to **B**. Bring the needle out at **C**, then slide it under the stitch from top to bottom.

2 Take the needle to the right of the loop and pass it under the diagonal stitch again. Bring it through over the working thread.

3 Pull the thread up to form a knot. Insert the needle at **D** and bring it out in line with **C** at **E**, ready to work the next stitch.

Chain

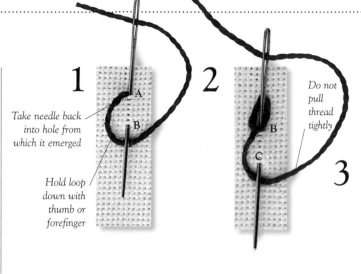

1 *Take needle back into hole from which it emerged*

A
B

Hold loop down with thumb or forefinger

2 *Do not pull thread tightly*

B
C

3 *Make loops all same length*

C
D
E

OTHER NAMES
*point de chainette;
Tambour stitch*

LEVEL
Easy

USES
*Straight lines and curves;
lettering; in rows
or spiral as filling*

METHOD
*Looped stitch, worked
from top to bottom*

MATERIALS
Any fabric; any thread

1 Start at **A**. Loop the thread from left to right and insert the needle again at **A**. Bring it through over the working thread at **B**.

2 Repeat step 1 to make the second stitch. Insert the needle inside the first loop at **B** and bring it out at **C**.

3 When the final stitch has been made, finish off by anchoring the last loop down with a small tie stitch (see p.20) from **D** to **E**.

Square Chain

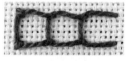

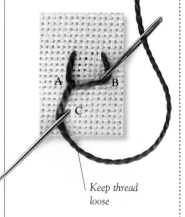

A   B
C

Keep thread loose

OTHER NAMES
*Ladder stitch; Roman
chain; open chain stitch*

LEVEL
Easy

USES
*Broad outlines; couching
stitch; foundation for
ribbon decoration;
traditional Indian
embroidery*

METHOD
*Looped stitch, worked
from top to bottom*

MATERIALS
Any fabric; any thread

Come out at **A**. Insert the needle inside the previous loop at **B**. Bring it through over the working thread at **C**, leaving an open loop. Repeat to continue. Anchor the final loop with a tie stitch (see p.20) at each corner.

Twisted Chain

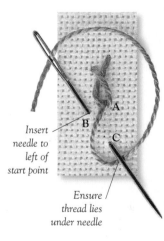

Insert needle to left of start point

A
B
C

Ensure thread lies under needle

LEVEL
Easy

USES
*Curved and textured
outlines*

METHOD
*Chain stitch variation
with crossed loop*

MATERIALS
*Any fabric; any thread –
non-stranded threads
give best effect*

Come up at **A**. Loop thread from left to right, insert the needle at **B**. Come up at **C**, pull through over the working thread. Repeat to continue. Finish with a tie stitch (see p.20) over the final loop.

Cable Chain

········· LEVEL ·········
Intermediate

········ METHOD ········
*Looped and twisted stitch,
worked from top
to bottom*

··········· USES ···········
*Decorative straight or
curved outlines*

······· MATERIALS ·······
*Any fabric; any thick
embroidery thread*

*Hold thread
to keep it taut*

1

*Hold thread down with
thumb or forefinger*

2

*Pull needle
over thread*

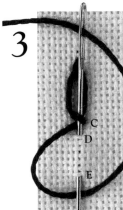

3

1 Start at **A**. Wrap the thread over and under the needle from left to right.

2 Insert the needle at **B**. Bring the point out at **C** over the working thread. Pull the needle through to form the first two links.

3 Twist the thread around the needle again and work the next stitch from **D** to **E**. Repeat steps 1 and 2 to continue stitching downwards.

Broad Chain

···· OTHER NAME ····
Reversed chain stitch

··········· LEVEL ···········
Intermediate

········ METHOD ········
*Looped stitch, worked
from top to bottom*

··········· USES ···········
Solid, flexible outline

······· MATERIALS ·······
*Any fabric;
firm embroidery thread*

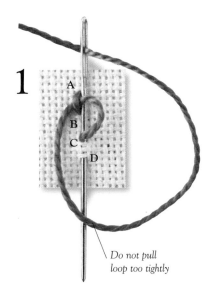

1

*Do not pull
loop too tightly*

2

*Work stitches close
together to create
solid chain*

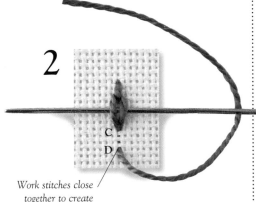

1 Start at **A** and make a short upright stitch to **B**. Come out directly below **B** at **C**, and slide the needle under the upright stitch from right to left. Take it down at **C**, pulling the thread gently to form the first loop. Bring the needle out again at **D**.

2 Pass the needle under both sides of the loop, then take it down at **D**. Repeat from **C** to continue.

Rope

········ LEVEL ········
Advanced

········ USES ········
Straight, curved or spiral outlines

······· MATERIALS ·······
Any fabric; any thick thread – stranded cotton gives a smooth effect; frame

··········· TIP ···········
Vary the angle of the stitches to work around a curve

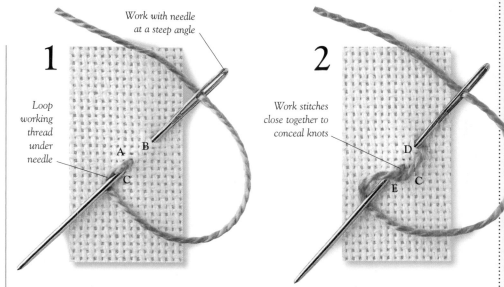

Work with needle at a steep angle

Loop working thread under needle

Work stitches close together to conceal knots

1 Start at **A**. Take the needle diagonally across and insert at **B**, then bring it up below and to the left of **A**, at **C**.

2 Pull the needle over the working thread to form a small knot at the base of the stitch. Insert the needle at **D** and bring it up at **E** to make the next stitch. Repeat this step to continue.

Scroll

······ OTHER NAME ······
Single knotted line stitch

········ LEVEL ········
Intermediate

·········· USES ··········
Decorative outlines

········ METHOD ········
Looped knot stitch

······· MATERIALS ·······
Any fabric; firm, non-stranded embroidery thread; frame

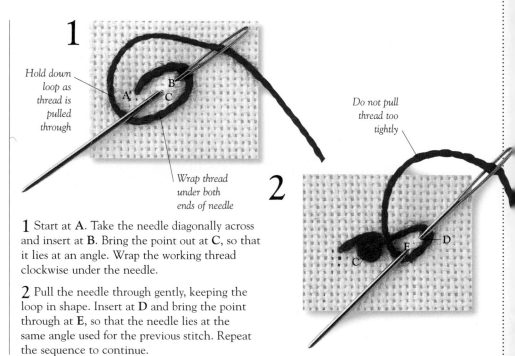

Hold down loop as thread is pulled through

Wrap thread under both ends of needle

Do not pull thread too tightly

1 Start at **A**. Take the needle diagonally across and insert at **B**. Bring the point out at **C**, so that it lies at an angle. Wrap the working thread clockwise under the needle.

2 Pull the needle through gently, keeping the loop in shape. Insert at **D** and bring the point through at **E**, so that the needle lies at the same angle used for the previous stitch. Repeat the sequence to continue.

Border Stitches

THIS IS THE largest, most widely used group of stitches and includes flat, looped and knotted techniques. Border stitches are used to create broad, decorative straight lines, frames, and edgings. They can be worked in straight or curved rows, singly as outlines or repeated to form a filling to cover a larger area. Use plainweave fabric for freestyle stitching or evenweave to produce the more regular stitches of counted thread work. Mount the fabric in a frame to prevent it puckering and to keep the stitches even, especially those such as herringbone which are made up of long straight stitches.

Paris

····· OTHER NAME ·····
Open square stitch

········· LEVEL ·········
Easy

··········· USES ···········
*Light border; in rows
as filling*

········ METHOD ········
*Back stitch variation with
upright branches*

····· MATERIALS ·····
*Evenweave fabric; any
thread*

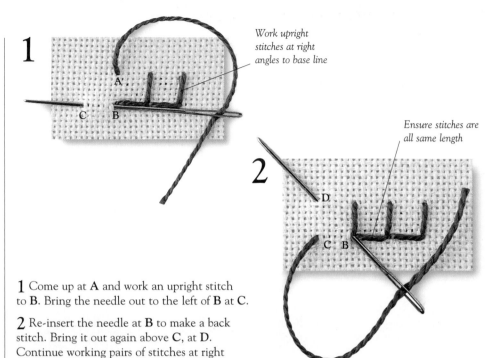

*Work upright
stitches at right
angles to base line*

*Ensure stitches are
all same length*

1 Come up at **A** and work an upright stitch
to **B**. Bring the needle out to the left of **B** at **C**.

2 Re-insert the needle at **B** to make a back
stitch. Bring it out again above **C**, at **D**.
Continue working pairs of stitches at right
angles in the same way.

Fern

····· OTHER NAME ·····
Fern leaf stitch

··········· LEVEL ···········
Easy

············· USES ·············
*Leaf veins and delicate
foliage sprays*

······ MATERIALS ······
Any fabric; any thread

·············· TIP ··············
*Vary length of stitches
when working on a curve*

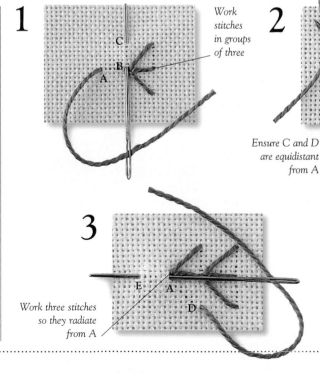

*Work
stitches
in groups
of three*

*Ensure C and D
are equidistant
from A*

*Work three stitches
so they radiate
from A*

1 Come out at **A**. Insert the
needle at **B** to make a horizontal
stitch. Come out directly above
B, at **C**.

2 Re-insert the needle at **A**
and bring it out below **C**, at **D**.

3 Insert the needle again at **A**
and come out at **E**, ready to
start the next group of stitches.

Bosnian

········ LEVEL ········
Easy

········ USES ··········
*Straight borders or
outlines; in rows as filling*

········ METHOD ········
*Worked horizontally in
two journeys*

······· MATERIALS ·······
Any fabric; any thread

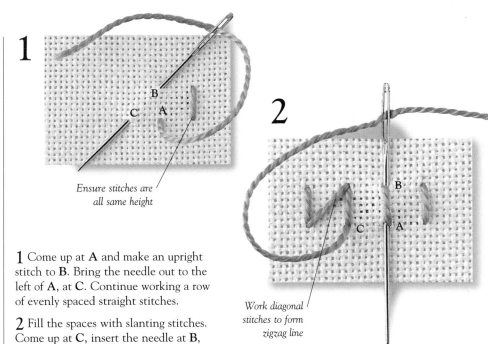

*Ensure stitches are
all same height*

*Work diagonal
stitches to form
zigzag line*

1 Come up at **A** and make an upright stitch to **B**. Bring the needle out to the left of **A**, at **C**. Continue working a row of evenly spaced straight stitches.

2 Fill the spaces with slanting stitches. Come up at **C**, insert the needle at **B**, then bring it out at **A**. Repeat to the end of the row.

Chevron

·········· LEVEL ··········
Easy

·········· USES ··········
*Straight border; in close
rows as light filling; in
smocking as surface
honeycomb stitch*

········ METHOD ········
*Worked horizontally
between parallel lines*

······· MATERIALS ·······
Any fabric; any thread

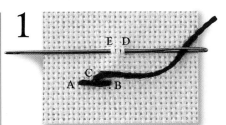

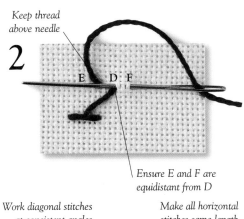

*Keep thread
above needle*

*Ensure E and F are
equidistant from D*

*Work diagonal stitches
at consistent angles*

*Make all horizontal
stitches same length*

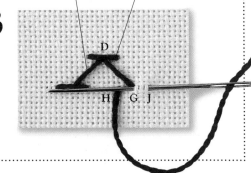

1 Start at **A** and make a horizontal straight stitch to **B**. Bring the needle out at the centre of the stitch, at **C**. Take the needle up to the right and insert it at **D**, then bring it out in line with **D**, at **E**.

2 Take the needle to the right and insert it at **F**. Come out again at **D**.

3 Take the needle down and insert at **G**, then come out at **H**. Insert the needle to the right, at **J**, and bring it out again at **G**. Repeat the sequence to continue.

Thorn

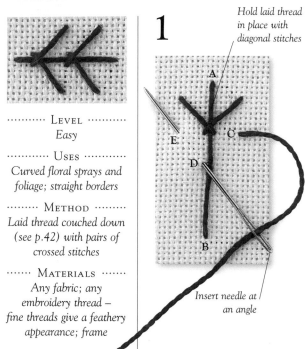

Hold laid thread in place with diagonal stitches

1

Insert needle at an angle

·········· LEVEL ··········
Easy

·········· USES ··········
Curved floral sprays and foliage; straight borders

········· METHOD ·········
Laid thread couched down (see p.42) with pairs of crossed stitches

········ MATERIALS ········
Any fabric; any embroidery thread – fine threads give a feathery appearance; frame

2

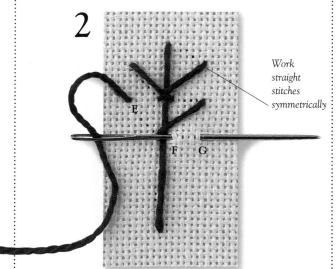

Work straight stitches symmetrically

1 Start at **A** and, following the line to be worked, make a long stitch to **B**. Use a second thread to work the couching stitches. Come up at **C** and take the needle across the laid thread to insert at **D**. Bring the needle out at **E**.

2 Insert the needle at **F** and bring it out at **G**, ready to make the next diagonal stitch. Make further pairs of stitches in the same way along the laid thread.

Cross

To work in rows:

1

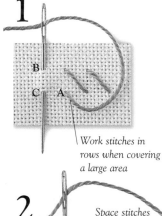

Work stitches in rows when covering a large area

·········· OTHER NAMES ··········
Berlin stitch; sampler stitch

·········· LEVEL ··········
Easy

·········· USES ··········
Geometric designs; charted patterns; lettering

········· METHOD ·········
Worked over equal number of horizontal and vertical threads

········ MATERIALS ········
Evenweave fabric; any embroidery thread

2

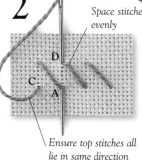

Space stitches evenly

Ensure top stitches all lie in same direction

1 Come up at **A**, insert the needle at **B** and come out at **C**. Repeat to make a series of evenly spaced diagonal stitches.

2 Work the top stitches in the opposite direction. Take the needle across from **C** and insert at **D**. Come out again at **A**. Repeat to complete the row.

To work stitches singly:

1   2

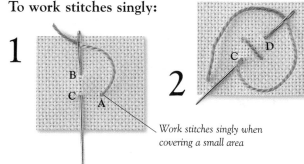

Work stitches singly when covering a small area

1 Start at **A**. Take the needle diagonally left and insert at **B**, then bring it out at **C**.

2 Insert the needle at **D** to complete the cross. Bring the needle out at **C** to work the next stitch.

Long-armed Cross

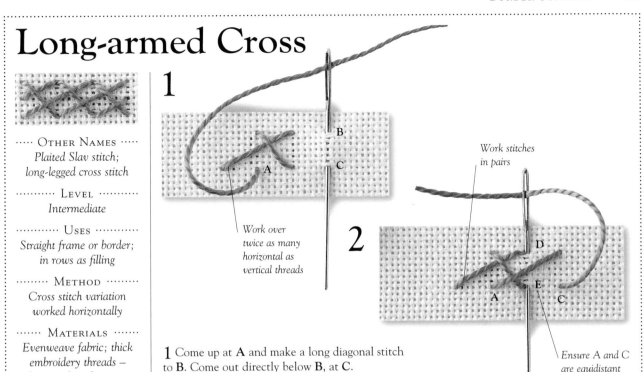

····· OTHER NAMES ·····
Plaited Slav stitch;
long-legged cross stitch

········ LEVEL ········
Intermediate

········ USES ·········
Straight frame or border;
in rows as filling

······· METHOD ·······
Cross stitch variation
worked horizontally

······ MATERIALS ·······
Evenweave fabric; thick
embroidery threads –
heavier threads give a
more raised appearance

Work over twice as many horizontal as vertical threads

Work stitches in pairs

Ensure A and C are equidistant from E

1 Come up at **A** and make a long diagonal stitch
to **B**. Come out directly below **B**, at **C**.

2 Take the needle back and insert at **D**, then bring it out directly
below, at **E**. Repeat these two steps to the end of the row.

Zigzag

········ LEVEL ········
Easy

········ USES ·········
Open outline; in close
rows as open filling

······· METHOD ·······
Alternate upright and
diagonal stitches, worked
horizontally in two
journeys

······ MATERIALS ·······
Any fabric; any thread –
fine twisted threads give
a more open effect

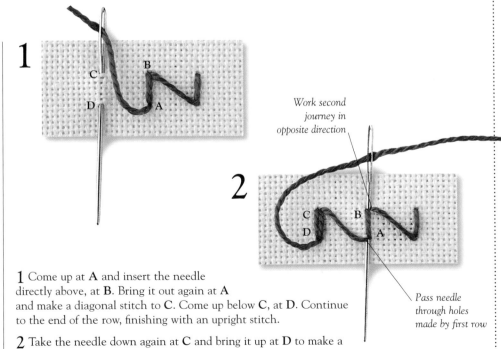

Work second journey in opposite direction

Pass needle through holes made by first row

1 Come up at **A** and insert the needle
directly above, at **B**. Bring it out again at **A**
and make a diagonal stitch to **C**. Come up below **C**, at **D**. Continue
to the end of the row, finishing with an upright stitch.

2 Take the needle down again at **C** and bring it up at **D** to make a
second upright stitch. Insert at **B** to make a diagonal stitch, then
come up at **A**. Repeat this step until all the crosses are complete.

Herringbone

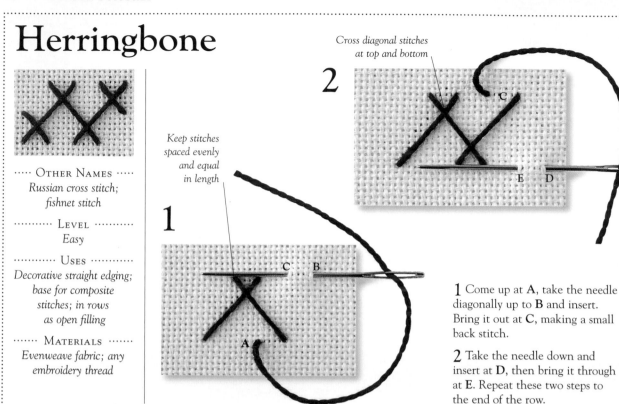

Cross diagonal stitches at top and bottom

Keep stitches spaced evenly and equal in length

2

1

····· OTHER NAMES ·····
*Russian cross stitch;
fishnet stitch*

········· LEVEL ·········
Easy

·········· USES ··········
*Decorative straight edging;
base for composite
stitches; in rows
as open filling*

····· MATERIALS ·····
*Evenweave fabric; any
embroidery thread*

1 Come up at **A**, take the needle diagonally up to **B** and insert. Bring it out at **C**, making a small back stitch.

2 Take the needle down and insert at **D**, then bring it through at **E**. Repeat these two steps to the end of the row.

Closed Herringbone

Stitches touch at top and bottom

2

1

······ OTHER NAME ······
Double back stitch

·········· LEVEL ··········
Intermediate

········· METHOD ·········
Herringbone variation

·········· USES ··········
*Open border; in rows as
lattice filling*

····· MATERIALS ·····
*Evenweave fabric; any
thread; frame*

1 Come up at **A** and make a diagonal stitch across to **B**. Bring the needle out on the same level, at **C**.

2 Take the needle down to **D** and insert, then come through at **E**. Repeat these two steps to continue.

·················· STITCH VARIATION ··················

Shadow stitch is formed when closed herringbone stitch is worked on the reverse side of a semi-transparent material. The design is outlined with back stitch and the crossed threads form a dense band of colour, which shows through the fabric. Mount fabric in a frame.

Basket

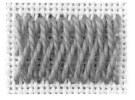

·········· LEVEL ··········
Advanced

·········· USES ··········
*Straight bands and
borders; in rows as a filling*

········ METHOD ········
*Alternate forward and
backward stitches, worked
downwards between two
parallel lines*

······· MATERIALS ·······
*Any fabric; stranded
thread gives a
smoother finish*

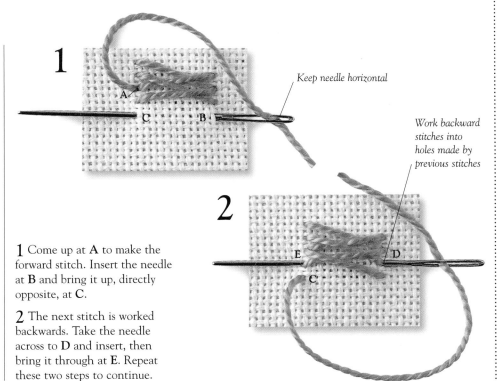

Keep needle horizontal

*Work backward
stitches into
holes made by
previous stitches*

1 Come up at **A** to make the
forward stitch. Insert the needle
at **B** and bring it up, directly
opposite, at **C**.

2 The next stitch is worked
backwards. Take the needle
across to **D** and insert, then
bring it through at **E**. Repeat
these two steps to continue.

Wheatear

·········· LEVEL ··········
Intermediate

·········· USES ··········
*Straight or gently curved
outlines; traditionally
worked on smocks
and childrens' clothes;
used singly as filling
(see p.81)*

········ METHOD ········
*Looped stitch, worked
from top to bottom*

······· MATERIALS ·······
*Any fabric; non-stranded
threads give raised effect*

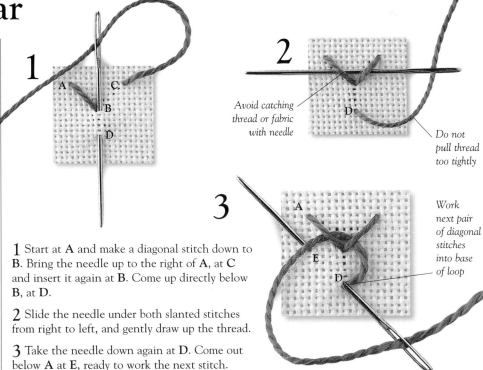

*Avoid catching
thread or fabric
with needle*

*Do not
pull thread
too tightly*

*Work
next pair
of diagonal
stitches
into base
of loop*

1 Start at **A** and make a diagonal stitch down to
B. Bring the needle up to the right of **A**, at **C**
and insert it again at **B**. Come up directly below
B, at **D**.

2 Slide the needle under both slanted stitches
from right to left, and gently draw up the thread.

3 Take the needle down again at **D**. Come out
below **A** at **E**, ready to work the next stitch.

Russian Chain

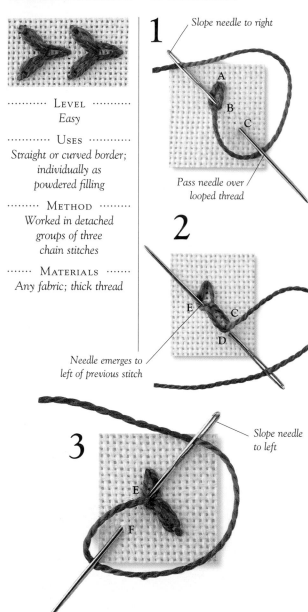

····· LEVEL ·····
Easy

····· USES ·····
*Straight or curved border;
individually as
powdered filling*

····· METHOD ·····
*Worked in detached
groups of three
chain stitches*

····· MATERIALS ·····
Any fabric; thick thread

1
Slope needle to right

A
B
C

Pass needle over
looped thread

2

E   C
D

Needle emerges to
left of previous stitch

3
Slope needle
to left

E
F

1 Work a chain stitch (see p.44) from **A** to **B**, bringing
the needle out to the right of centre. Insert again at **B**, loop
the thread from left to right and bring the needle out at **C**.

2 Insert the needle at **D** to make a tie stitch (see p.20),
then bring the needle up inside the first loop, at **E**.

3 Make the third chain stitch at an angle from **E** to **F** in
the same way. Finish with a tie stitch. Work the next and
subsequent groups of stitches directly below the first.

Petal

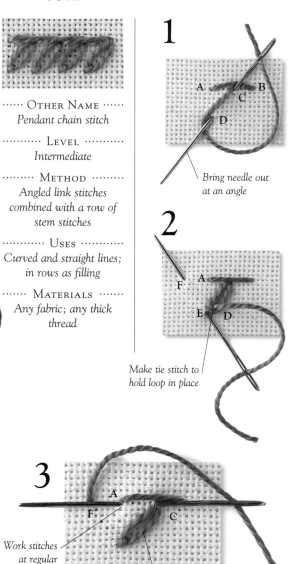

····· OTHER NAME ·····
Pendant chain stitch

····· LEVEL ·····
Intermediate

····· METHOD ·····
*Angled link stitches
combined with a row of
stem stitches*

····· USES ·····
*Curved and straight lines;
in rows as filling*

····· MATERIALS ·····
*Any fabric; any thick
thread*

1

A   B
C
D

Bring needle out
at an angle

2

F   A
E   D

Make tie stitch to
hold loop in place

3

A
F   C

Work stitches
at regular
intervals

Ensure loops are
same length

1 Start at **A** and make a straight stitch to **B**. Bring the
needle up at the centre of the stitch at **C**. Work a chain
stitch (see p.44) from **C** to **D**.

2 Insert the needle at **E** to make a tie stitch (see p.20).
Come out to the left of **A** at **F**.

3 Insert the needle again at the top of the loop, at **C**, and
come out at **A**, ready to make the next pair of stitches.

Zigzag Chain

OTHER NAME
Vandyke chain

LEVEL
Intermediate

USES
Straight and gently curved lines and outlines

METHOD
Chain stitches worked at alternate angles

MATERIALS
Any fabric; twisted thread; sharp needle

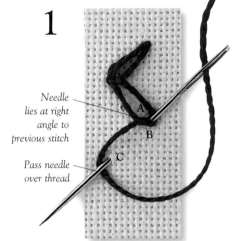

1

Needle lies at right angle to previous stitch

Pass needle over thread

1 Come up inside the previous stitch at **A**. Loop the thread from left to right and insert the needle at **B** so that it pierces the base of the stitch. Bring the needle out at **C**, over the working thread.

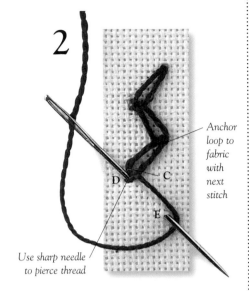

2

Anchor loop to fabric with next stitch

Use sharp needle to pierce thread

2 Loop the thread from right to left and insert the needle at **D**, through the base of the last stitch. Come out at **E** and continue making stitches at right angles. Finish off with a tie stitch (see p.20) over the final loop.

Rosette Chain

OTHER NAME
Bead edging stitch

LEVEL
Advanced

USES
Straight or curved borders

METHOD
Twisted chain variation, worked horizontally

MATERIALS
Any fabric; thick non-stranded thread

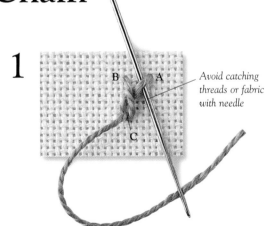

1

Avoid catching threads or fabric with needle

1 Start at **A**. Loop the thread from left to right and insert the needle at **B**. Come up at **C** and pull the needle through the loop. Slide the needle under the thread to the left of **A** from bottom to top, and pull through gently.

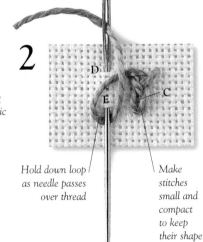

2

Hold down loop as needle passes over thread

Make stitches small and compact to keep their shape

2 Insert the needle at **D** and come up through the loop at **E**, as before. Repeat to continue.

·········TECHNIQUE VARIATION·········

Work rosette chain in a circle to create a petalled flower motif. The stitches radiate from a central point and should be evenly spaced.

Loop

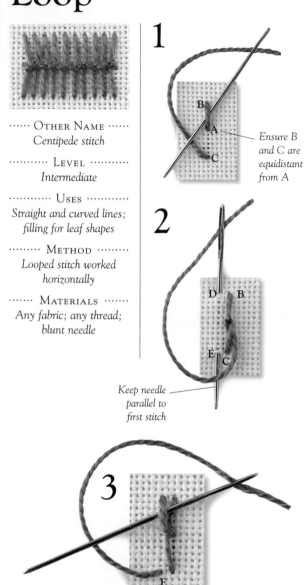

····· OTHER NAME ·····
Centipede stitch

········ LEVEL ········
Intermediate

········ USES ··········
*Straight and curved lines;
filling for leaf shapes*

······· METHOD ········
*Looped stitch worked
horizontally*

······ MATERIALS ······
*Any fabric; any thread;
blunt needle*

Ensure B and C are equidistant from A

Keep needle parallel to first stitch

1 Start at **A**. Make an upright stitch to **B**, then come out directly below **A**, at **C**. Slide the needle under the stitch from right to left, over the working thread.

2 Insert the needle level with **B** at **D**. Come up at **E**, keeping the needle below the working thread.

3 Pass the needle under the previous stitch from right to left, over the working thread. Repeat steps 2 and 3 to continue. Finish off by taking the thread through to the back at the centre of the final stitch.

Flat Vandyke

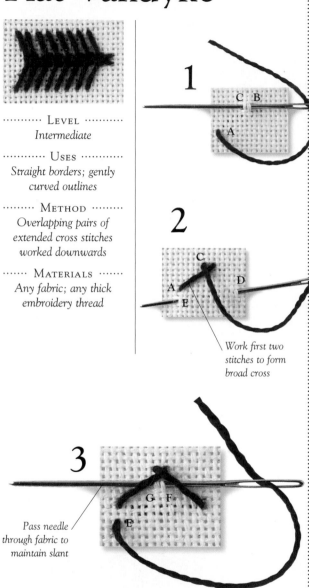

········ LEVEL ········
Intermediate

········ USES ··········
*Straight borders; gently
curved outlines*

······· METHOD ········
*Overlapping pairs of
extended cross stitches
worked downwards*

······ MATERIALS ······
*Any fabric; any thick
embroidery thread*

Work first two stitches to form broad cross

Pass needle through fabric to maintain slant

1 Start at **A**. Make a diagonal stitch up to **B** and bring the needle out to the left of **B**, at **C**.

2 Take the needle down and insert level with **A**, at **D**. Come up below **A**, at **E**.

3 Pass the needle under the crossed stitches from **F** to **G**, picking up two threads of background fabric. Repeat steps 2 and 3 to continue.

Ladder

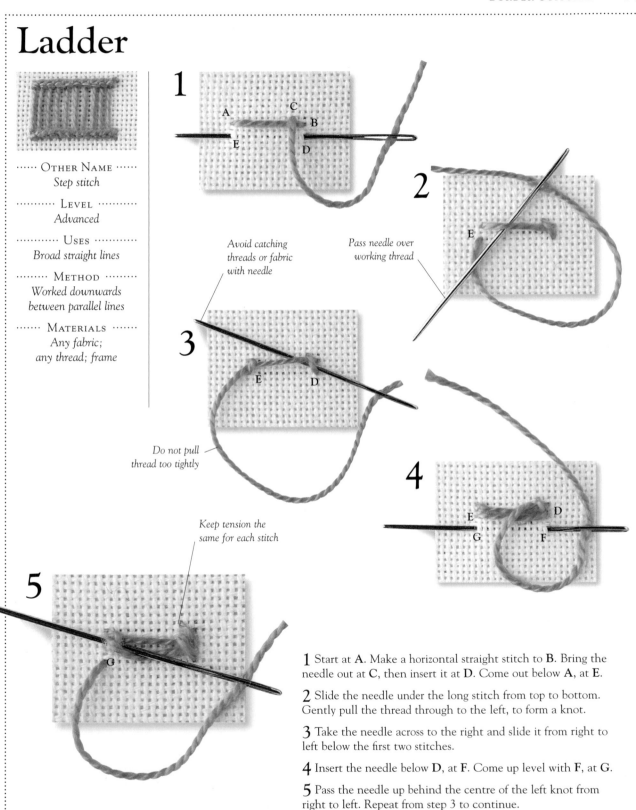

Other Name
Step stitch

Level
Advanced

Uses
Broad straight lines

Method
*Worked downwards
between parallel lines*

Materials
*Any fabric;
any thread; frame*

*Avoid catching
threads or fabric
with needle*

*Pass needle over
working thread*

*Do not pull
thread too tightly*

*Keep tension the
same for each stitch*

1 Start at **A**. Make a horizontal straight stitch to **B**. Bring the needle out at **C**, then insert it at **D**. Come out below **A**, at **E**.

2 Slide the needle under the long stitch from top to bottom. Gently pull the thread through to the left, to form a knot.

3 Take the needle across to the right and slide it from right to left below the first two stitches.

4 Insert the needle below **D**, at **F**. Come up level with **F**, at **G**.

5 Pass the needle up behind the centre of the left knot from right to left. Repeat from step 3 to continue.

Blanket

······ OTHER NAME ······
Open buttonhole stitch

········· LEVEL ·········
Easy

········ METHOD ········
*Looped stitch, worked
horizontally*

·········· USES ··········
*Straight or curved borders
and outlines; finishing
edges; securing appliqué
shapes; filling (see p.87)*

······· MATERIALS ·······
*Woven fabrics or felt; any
wool or thread*

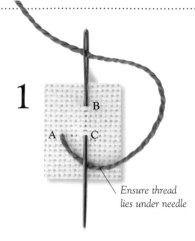

*Ensure thread
lies under needle*

1 Start at **A**. Take the needle up and insert
at **B**, then bring it out directly below and
level with **A**, at **C**.

2 Pull the needle down over the working
thread. Insert the needle at **D** then bring it
out at **E** to make the next stitch. Repeat this
step to continue. Finish off with a tie stitch
(see p.20) over the final loop.

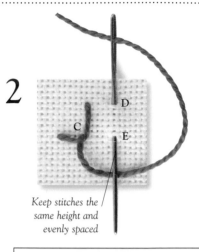

*Keep stitches the
same height and
evenly spaced*

······· STITCH VARIATION ·······

Buttonhole stitch is
worked in the same
way but the stitches lie
next to each other to
create a solid line. The background fabric is
completely covered and will not fray, so it is
ideal for cutwork (see pp112-113), and
neatening hems and hand-worked buttonholes.

Closed Buttonhole

·········· LEVEL ··········
Easy

········· METHOD ·········
*Triangular blanket
stitch variation, worked
horizontally*

·········· USES ··········
*Decorative edgings and
borders; in rows as filling*

········ MATERIALS ········
Any fabric; any thread

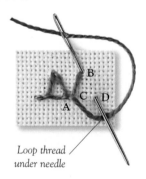

*Loop thread
under needle*

Come up at **A** and insert
the needle at **B**. Bring it up
close to **A**, at **C**. Pull the
needle over the working
thread. Re-insert at **B** and
come up to the right at **D**.
Pull the needle over the
loop. Repeat to continue.

Single Feather

·········· LEVEL ··········
Easy

········· METHOD ·········
*Blanket stitch variation,
worked downwards*

·········· USES ··········
*Decorative edging;
outlines and borders;
in smocking; in rows
as open filling*

······· MATERIALS ·······
*Any fabric;
any embroidery thread*

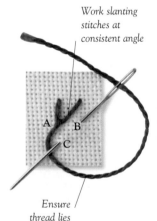

*Work slanting
stitches at
consistent angle*

*Ensure
thread lies
under needle*

Come up at **A**. Take the
needle across to the right
and insert it at **B**. Come out
below **A**, at **C**. Pull the
needle over the working
thread. Repeat to continue.

Up and Down Buttonhole

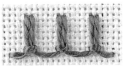

.... LEVEL ....
Intermediate

.... METHOD ....
*Buttonhole stitch
variation, worked
alternately upwards
and downwards*

.... USES ....
*Straight or curved lines
and edgings; in rows
as filling*

.... MATERIALS ....
*Any fabric; any
embroidery thread*

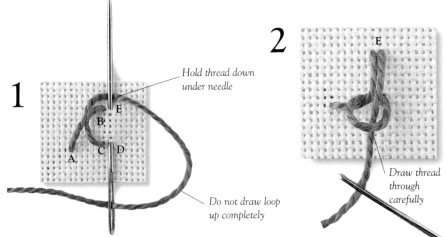

*Hold thread down
under needle*

*Do not draw loop
up completely*

*Draw thread
through
carefully*

1 Start at **A**. Insert the needle at **B** and bring it out at **C**, as for step 1 of blanket stitch (see left). Insert the needle at **D** and bring it out at **E**, ensuring that the working thread lies under the point. Pull the needle upwards, so that the thread forms a loose loop.

2 Take the needle downwards, pulling gently until the loop tightens around the base of the two upright stitches. Repeat these two steps to continue.

Open Cretan

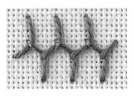

.... LEVEL ....
Easy

.... METHOD ....
*Looped stitch worked
from top to bottom*

.... USES ....
*Curved or straight lines;
open filling*

.... MATERIALS ....
*Any fabric; any thread –
finer threads give a lacy
appearance; frame*

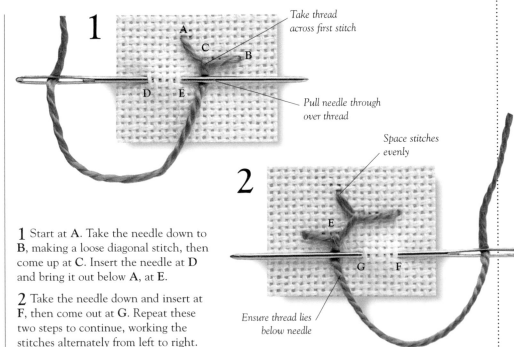

*Take thread
across first stitch*

*Pull needle through
over thread*

*Space stitches
evenly*

*Ensure thread lies
below needle*

1 Start at **A**. Take the needle down to **B**, making a loose diagonal stitch, then come up at **C**. Insert the needle at **D** and bring it out below **A**, at **E**.

2 Take the needle down and insert at **F**, then come out at **G**. Repeat these two steps to continue, working the stitches alternately from left to right.

Feather

····· OTHER NAMES ·····
Briar stitch;
single coral stitch

········· LEVEL ·········
Easy

········· USES ··········
Smocking; hems;
crazy patchwork; with
ribbon embroidery

········ METHOD ········
Looped stitch, worked
alternately from left to right
in straight or curved lines

······· MATERIALS ·······
Any fabric; any thread

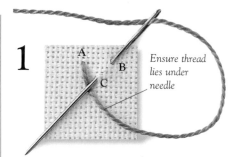

1 *Ensure thread lies under needle*

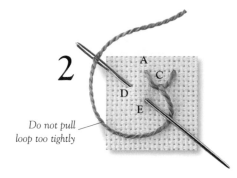

2 *Do not pull loop too tightly*

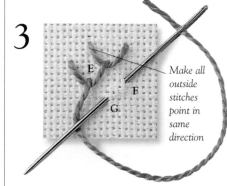

3 *Make all outside stitches point in same direction*

1 Start at **A** and insert the needle to the right, at **B**, leaving a thread loop. Bring the point out over the thread at **C** and pull through.

2 Insert the needle to the left of **C**, at **D**. Come out directly below **A**, at **E**, and pull through over the loop.

3 Insert the needle at **F** and bring it out at **G**, over the loop. Repeat steps 2 and 3 to continue. Finish off with a tie stitch (see p.20) over the final loop.

Closed Feather

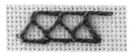

········· LEVEL ·········
Easy

········· USES ··········
Straight lines and
borders; in rows
as open filling

········ METHOD ········
Feather variation
worked downwards

······· MATERIALS ·······
Any fabric;
thick threads will
give a textured effect

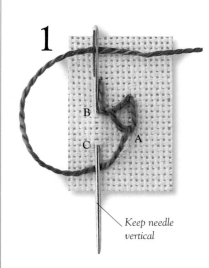

1 *Keep needle vertical*

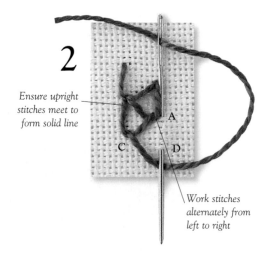

2 *Ensure upright stitches meet to form solid line*

Work stitches alternately from left to right

1 Come up at **A**. Take the needle diagonally up to the left and insert at **B**. Bring the point out over the working thread at **C** and pull through.

2 Re-insert the needle at **A**, bring it out at **D** and pull through over the working thread. Repeat these two steps to continue. Finish off with a tie stitch (see p.20) over the last loop.

Double Feather

····· OTHER NAME ·····
Thorn and briar stitch

········· LEVEL ·········
Easy

·········· USES ··········
*Foliage and branches;
decorating children's
garments*

······· METHOD ·······
*Looped stitch,
worked alternately
from left to right*

······ MATERIALS ······
*Any fabric; fine thread will
give a lacy effect*

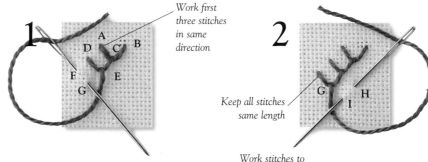

*Work first
three stitches
in same
direction*

*Keep all stitches
same length*

*Work stitches to
form a broad zigzag*

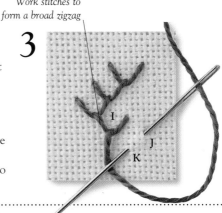

1 Work the first two stitches as for feather stitch (see p.60), then make a second stitch to the left. Insert the needle level with **E** at **F**, and come out at **G**. Pull the needle through over the loop.

2 Take the needle across to the right and insert at **H**. Come out at **I** and pull through over the loop.

3 Make a second stitch to the right; take the needle down at **J**, bring it out at **K** and pull through over the loop. Continue working downwards, making two stitches one side, then the other.

Chained Feather

····· OTHER NAMES ·····
Feathered chain stitch

········· LEVEL ·········
Intermediate

·········· USES ··········
Decorative borders; foliage

······· METHOD ·······
*Row of slanting picot
stitches set at
alternate angles*

······ MATERIALS ······
Any fabric; any thread

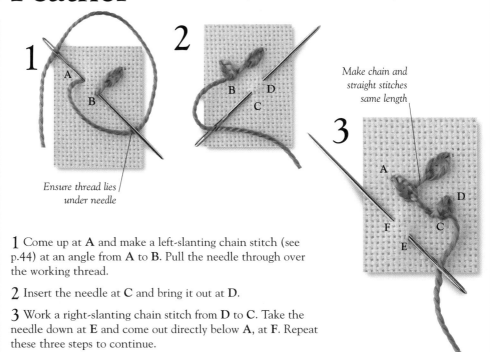

*Ensure thread lies
under needle*

*Make chain and
straight stitches
same length*

1 Come up at **A** and make a left-slanting chain stitch (see p.44) at an angle from **A** to **B**. Pull the needle through over the working thread.

2 Insert the needle at **C** and bring it out at **D**.

3 Work a right-slanting chain stitch from **D** to **C**. Take the needle down at **E** and come out directly below **A**, at **F**. Repeat these three steps to continue.

Composite Border Stitches

THIS IS THE most decorative group of stitches which can be worked in single rows, or repeated to create multi-coloured fillings with intricate surface textures. Basic outline and border stitches are embellished with interlacing to create some of them, and others are a combination of two or even three stitches. Magic and Singalese chain are flexible stitches which can be sewn along a curved line, but the rest are all made in straight rows. Use a blunt needle for any interlacing and mount the fabric in an embroidery frame, so that the stitches do not become distorted.

Pekinese

····· Other Names ·····
Chinese stitch;
forbidden stitch

········· Level ·········
Easy

········· Uses ·········
Decorative curved and
straight outlines; in rows
as filling

········ Method ········
Laced back stitch, worked
horizontally

····· Materials ·····
Any fabric; lacing can be
worked in thicker thread;
blunt needle

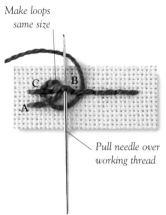

Make loops
same size

Pull needle over
working thread

Work a row of back stitch
(see p.40). Bring the lacing
thread out at **A**. Slide the
needle upwards beneath **B**,
then pass it downwards under
C. Draw the thread up gently
and continue lacing to the
end of the row.

Laced Buttonhole

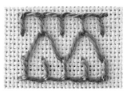

····· Other Name ·····
Threaded buttonhole stitch

········· Level ·········
Easy

········· Uses ·········
Decorative straight
edgings and borders

········ Method ········
Two rows of blanket stitch
with interlacing

····· Materials ·····
Any fabric; any thread
in two colours; frame;
blunt needle

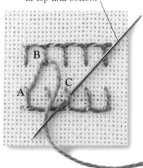

Lace under
alternate stitches
at top and bottom

Work two parallel rows of
blanket stitch (see p.58) with
the upright stitches pointing
inwards. Bring the lacing
thread out at **A**. Slide the
needle under **B**, then beneath
C. Continue lacing to the end
of the row.

Interlacing Band

····· Other Names ·····
Double Pekinese stitch;
herringbone ladder stitch

········· Level ·········
Intermediate

··········· Uses ···········
Braided straight lines

········ Method ········
Two rows of back stitch
with looped interlacing

····· Materials ·····
Any fabric; any two
threads in the same or
different thicknesses;
frame; blunt needle

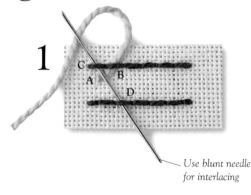

1

Use blunt needle
for interlacing

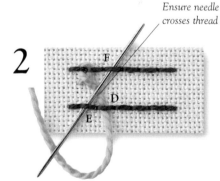

2

Ensure needle
crosses thread

1 Work two parallel lines of back stitch (see
p.40), starting the bottom row with a half-length
stitch. Bring the lacing thread out at **A**. Pass the
needle upwards beneath **B**, then slide it
downwards under both **C** and **D**.

2 Take the needle to the left and slide it under **E**
and **F**, then pull through. Continue lacing up and
down to the end of the row.

········· Technique Variation ·········

To create a wider, more
open border, work the
twisted interlacing over
two rows of blanket
stitch (see p.58), again
using two colours.

Magic Chain

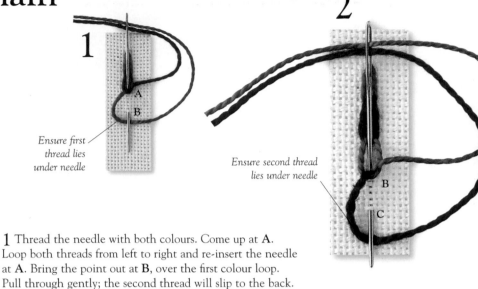

1

Ensure first thread lies under needle

2

Ensure second thread lies under needle

A

B

B

C

····· OTHER NAMES ·····
Chequered chain stitch; two-coloured chain stitch

········ LEVEL ········
Intermediate

········ USES ········
Straight or curved outlines

········ METHOD ········
Chain stitch variation worked with two threads

····· MATERIALS ·····
Any fabric; two contrasting threads in the same weight; long-eyed needle

1 Thread the needle with both colours. Come up at **A**. Loop both threads from left to right and re-insert the needle at **A**. Bring the point out at **B**, over the first colour loop. Pull through gently; the second thread will slip to the back.

2 Loop the threads from left to right and re-insert the needle at **B**. Bring the point out at **C**, over the second colour loop: pull through. Repeat the steps to the end of the row. Finish with a tie stitch (see p.20) over the last loop.

Singalese Chain

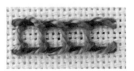

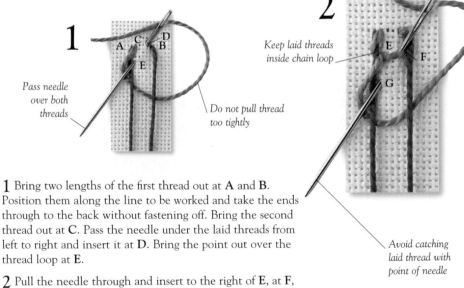

1

A C D B

E

Pass needle over both threads

Do not pull thread too tightly

2

Keep laid threads inside chain loop

E

F

G

Avoid catching laid thread with point of needle

········ LEVEL ········
Advanced

········ USES ········
Decorative borders; curved or straight outlines; casing for narrow ribbon

········ METHOD ········
Square chain stitch worked downwards over contrasting threads

····· MATERIALS ·····
Any fabric; any two different coloured threads of equal weight

1 Bring two lengths of the first thread out at **A** and **B**. Position them along the line to be worked and take the ends through to the back without fastening off. Bring the second thread out at **C**. Pass the needle under the laid threads from left to right and insert it at **D**. Bring the point out over the thread loop at **E**.

2 Pull the needle through and insert to the right of **E**, at **F**, then bring it out at **G**, ready to work the next stitch. Repeat this step to continue, easing the laid threads into position. Fasten down the final loop with two tie stitches (see p.20) and finish off the laid threads on the reverse side.

Threaded Chain

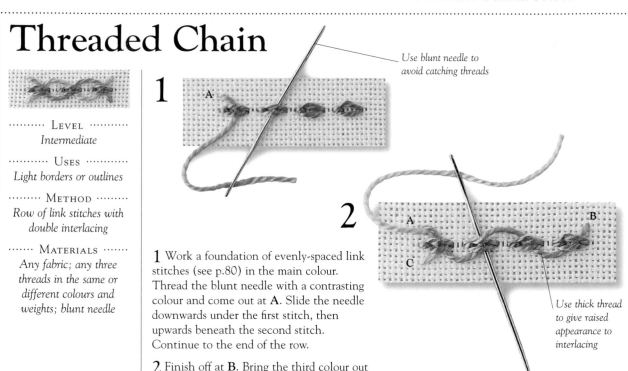

.... LEVEL ....
Intermediate

.... USES ....
Light borders or outlines

.... METHOD ....
*Row of link stitches with
double interlacing*

...... MATERIALS ......
*Any fabric; any three
threads in the same or
different colours and
weights; blunt needle*

*Use blunt needle to
avoid catching threads*

*Use thick thread
to give raised
appearance to
interlacing*

1 Work a foundation of evenly-spaced link stitches (see p.80) in the main colour. Thread the blunt needle with a contrasting colour and come out at **A**. Slide the needle downwards under the first stitch, then upwards beneath the second stitch. Continue to the end of the row.

2 Finish off at **B**. Bring the third colour out at **C** and lace it alternately up and down under the link stitches, filling in the spaces.

Guilloche

.... LEVEL ....
Advanced

.... USES ....
*Multi-coloured straight
borders and edgings*

.... METHOD ....
*Combination of stem and
satin stitches with French
knots and interlacing*

...... MATERIALS ......
*Evenweave fabric;
thick thread in three
colours; blunt needle*

*Work out positions
of each line and
group of stitches
before beginning*

*Use blunt
needle to avoid
catching threads*

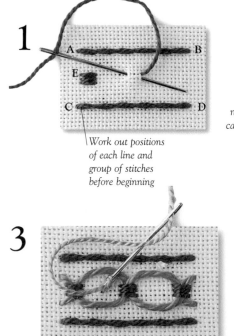

1 Using the main colour, work two parallel lines of stem stitch (see p.41) from **A** to **B** and from **C** to **D**. Work groups of three short satin stitches (see p.86) at regular intervals between the lines, starting at **E**.

2 Interlace the satin stitches with contrasting threads as for threaded chain stitch (see above).

3 Finish off by working a French knot (see p.76) in the centre of each loop, using the third thread.

Raised Chevron

······· LEVEL ·······
Intermediate

········ USES ·········
*Straight outlines
and light borders*

········ METHOD ········
*Chevron stitch worked
over two lines of
arrowhead stitches*

······· MATERIALS ·······
*Any fabric; thicker thread
gives more
texture – choose two
contrasting colours*

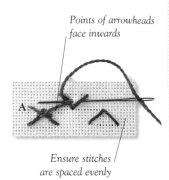

*Points of arrowheads
face inwards*

*Ensure stitches
are spaced evenly*

Stitch two parallel rows of arrowheads (see p.73) in the first colour. Bring the second thread out at **A** and work a band of chevron stitch (see p.49) from left to right, so that the horizontal stitches lie across the points of the arrowhead stitches.

Backstitched Herringbone

········ LEVEL ········
Easy

········ USES ·········
*Open borders; in rows
as a lattice filling*

········ METHOD ········
*Herringbone stitch with
back stitch detail*

······· MATERIALS ·······
*Any fabric; two
contrasting threads in the
same or different weights*

*Work back stitches
over crossed threads*

Work a line of herringbone stitch (see p.52). Using the second thread, make a back stitch from **A** to **B**. Bring the needle up at **C**, insert at **D**, and come out at **E**. Continue to the end of the row.

Raised Lattice Band

········ LEVEL ·········
Advanced

········· USES ··········
Decorative borders

········ METHOD ·········
*Interlaced herringbone
stitch worked over
padded satin stitch*

······· MATERIALS ·······
*Any fabric; lustrous
thread in three colours;
blunt needle; frame*

1

*Work upright
stitches close
together*

2

*Ensure lacing is not
pulled too tightly*

3

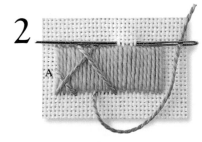

1 Work a foundation of long horizontal surface satin stitch (see p.86). Work a row of upright satin (see p.86) from left to right over the base stitches.

2 Bring the second thread up at **A** and work a row of herringbone stitch (see p.52).

3 Thread the blunt needle with the third colour thread. Come up at **A** and slide the needle upwards, under the centre of the first long diagonal stitch. Take it back down under the second stitch from top to bottom. Continue lacing to the end of the band.

Double Herringbone

····· OTHER NAME ·····
Indian herringbone stitch

········· LEVEL ·········
Advanced

········· USES ·········
*Geometric border; in rows
as open filling*

········ METHOD ········
*Two interlaced rows of
herringbone stitch*

······· MATERIALS ·······
*Any fabric; any thick
thread in two colours*

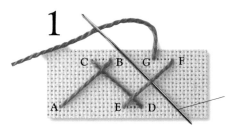

Slide needle
under previous
stitch

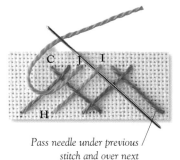

Pass needle under previous
stitch and over next

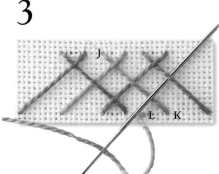

1 Start at **A** and make a diagonal stitch to **B**. Bring the needle out at **C**, pass it under the stitch and take it down at **D**. Come out at **E** and insert at **F**. Bring the needle out at **G** and slide it under the last stitch. Continue to the end of the row.

2 Bring the contrast thread up directly below **C**, at **H**. Slide the needle under the second stitch and insert at **I**. Come out at **J** and pass the needle under the previous stitch.

3 Insert the needle at **K** and come out at **L**. Take it over the first thread and under the second. Repeat steps 2 and 3 to continue.

Twisted Lattice Band

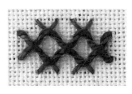

········· LEVEL ·········
Advanced

········· USES ·········
*Ornamental border; in
rows as filling*

········ METHOD ········
*Double herringbone stitch
with two rows of
interlacing*

······· MATERIALS ·······
*Any fabric; any thick
thread in two colours*

Do not pull lacing
thread too tightly

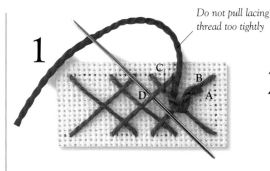

Always pass needle
under stitch

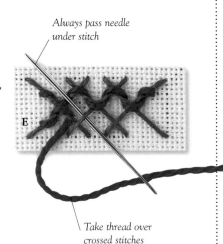

Take thread over
crossed stitches

1 Work a foundation of double herringbone stitch (see above) in the first colour. Bring the lacing thread out at **A**. Pass the needle downwards under **B**, then upwards under **C**. Slide it beneath the next stitch, at **D**, from top to bottom.

2 Continue weaving the thread under and over the top stitches to the end of the row. Bring the thread out at **E** and interlace the bottom stitches in the same way to complete.

Butterfly Chain

········· LEVEL ·········
Intermediate

········· USES ·········
Light frames or borders

········ METHOD ········
*Twisted chain stitch
worked over groups of
three straight stitches,
without piercing fabric*

······· MATERIALS ·······
*Any fabric; thick thread in
two colours; blunt needle*

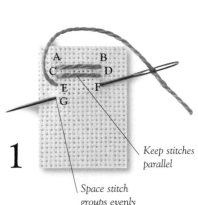

1

*Keep stitches
parallel*

*Space stitch
groups evenly*

2

*Pass needle over
working thread*

1 Start at **A**, and make a horizontal stitch across to **B**. Work two more stitches directly below, from **C** to **D** and **E** to **F**, then bring the needle out at **G** to work the next group of three stitches.

2 Using the contrast thread, work a twisted chain stitch (see p.44) over each group of horizontal stitches. Come through at **A** and loop the thread to the right. Slide the needle under all three stitches and pull it through. Tighten the thread to draw the stitches together.

Raised Chain Band

····· OTHER NAME ·····
Raised chain stitch

········· LEVEL ·········
Intermediate

········· USES ·········
Heavy borders

········ METHOD ········
*Chain stitch worked over
straight stitch foundation,
without piercing fabric*

······ MATERIALS ······
*Any fabric; any thick
thread in two colours;
blunt needle*

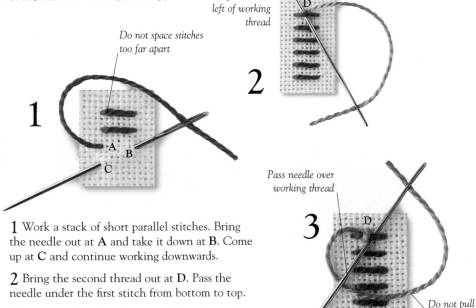

*Keep needle to
left of working
thread*

*Do not space stitches
too far apart*

1

2

*Pass needle over
working thread*

3

*Do not pull
thread up
too tightly*

1 Work a stack of short parallel stitches. Bring the needle out at **A** and take it down at **B**. Come up at **C** and continue working downwards.

2 Bring the second thread out at **D**. Pass the needle under the first stitch from bottom to top.

3 Loop the thread to the right. Slide the needle downwards under the first stitch, to the right of **D**. Repeat steps 2 and 3 to the end of the stack.

FILLING STITCHES

POWDERED FILLING AND
ISOLATED STITCHES

OPEN AND SOLID
FILLING STITCHES

Powdered Filling and Isolated Stitches

THESE DETACHED STITCHES are all worked singly and vary considerably in size. The larger versions are often used as accent stitches, while the smaller ones are repeated to form a powdered filling. The stitches can be arranged in several ways: in regular rows to form straight lines and geometric patterns; scattered randomly; spaced apart to allow the background fabric to show through, or sewn close together to form a dense, textured surface. A design usually requires a powdered filling to be contained within an area which has been defined with an outline or border stitch.

Straight **73**	Fly **78**
Arrowhead **73**	Sheaf Filling **78**
Dot **73**	Crown **78**
St George Cross **73**	Sorbello **79**
Ermine **74**	Palestrina Knot **79**
Square Boss **74**	Link **80**
Star **74**	Lazy Daisy **80**
Woven Star **75**	Berry **80**
Woven Cross **75**	Picot **80**
French Knot **76**	Detached Wheatear **81**
Pistil **76**	Tulip **81**
Bullion Knot **76**	Woven Spider Web **82**
Danish Knot **77**	Ribbon Rose **82**
Four-legged Knot **77**	Ribbed Web **82**
Sword **77**	Buttonhole Wheel **82**
Shisha **83**	

Straight

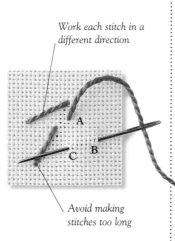

Work each stitch in a different direction

Avoid making stitches too long

····· OTHER NAME ·····
Stroke stitch

········ LEVEL ········
Easy

·········· USES ··········
Foliage; textured filling

······· METHOD ·······
Randomly placed single stitches of varying length

····· MATERIALS ·····
Any fabric; any thread

Come up at **A**. Take the needle down to **B** and insert, then bring it out at **C**. Continue working straight stitches in a random pattern to fill the required area.

Arrowhead

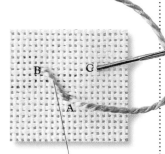

Slanting stitches form 'V' shape

········ LEVEL ········
Easy

·········· USES ··········
Powdered filling; worked in vertical or horizontal rows as border stitch

······· METHOD ·······
Two straight stitches worked at a right angle

····· MATERIALS ·····
Any fabric; thick threads create raised effect

Start at **A**. Make a diagonal straight stitch up to **B**, then come out again at **A**. Insert the needle at **C** to complete.

Dot

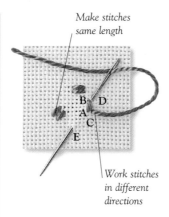

Make stitches same length

Work stitches in different directions

····· OTHER NAME ·····
Backstitched seeding

········ LEVEL ········
Easy

·········· USES ··········
Powdered filling; worked in rows as outline

······· METHOD ·······
Pairs of short, closely spaced back stitches

····· MATERIALS ·····
Any fabric; pearl thread makes stitches stand out

Come up at **A**. Insert the needle at **B** and bring it out at **C**. Insert at **D** to complete the second stitch, then bring the needle up at **E** to work the next pair of stitches.

St George Cross

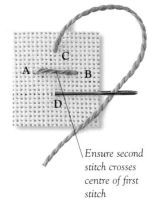

Ensure second stitch crosses centre of first stitch

····· OTHER NAME ·····
Upright cross stitch

········ LEVEL ········
Easy

·········· USES ··········
Geometric or random fillings; isolated stitch

····· MATERIALS ·····
Any fabric; twisted threads give raised effect

Start at **A** and work a horizontal straight stitch across to **B**. Come out at **C**. Take the needle down over the first stitch and insert at **D** to complete the cross.

Ermine

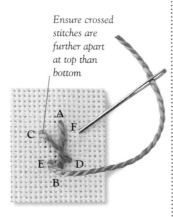

Ensure crossed stitches are further apart at top than bottom

········ LEVEL ········
Easy

········ USES ········
Scattered or regular filling; in rows as border; isolated stitch; in blackwork

········ METHOD ········
Wide cross stitch worked over upright straight stitch

········ MATERIALS ········
Evenweave fabric for a regular effect; any thread

Start at **A** and work a vertical straight stitch to **B**. Bring the needle out at **C** and insert at **D**. Come out at **E**. Take the needle across the two stitches and insert at **F** to complete.

Square Boss

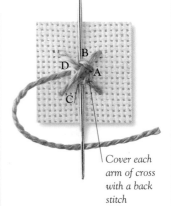

Cover each arm of cross with a back stitch

····· OTHER NAME ·····
Raised knot

········ LEVEL ········
Intermediate

········ USES ········
Light fillings; in rows as border; isolated stitch

········ METHOD ········
Cross stitch covered by back stitch square

········ MATERIALS ········
Any fabric; thick thread gives raised texture

Make a cross stitch (see p.50). Bring the needle out at **A** and take it down at **B**. Come out at **C** and insert at **A**. Bring the needle out at **D** and insert at **C**. Work a back stitch from **B** to **D** to complete.

Star

········ LEVEL ········
Intermediate

········ USES ········
Scattered as light filling; in rows as border; isolated stitch

········ METHOD ········
Elongated cross stitch worked over St George cross and cross stitches

········ MATERIALS ········
Any fabric; any thread

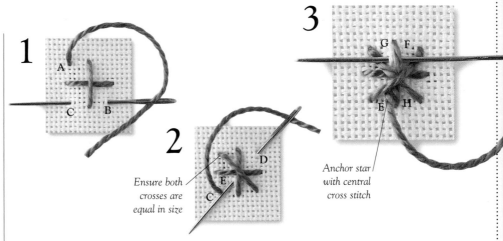

Ensure both crosses are equal in size

Anchor star with central cross stitch

1 Make a St George cross stitch (see p.73). Bring the needle out at **A**, and work a diagonal stitch down to **B**. Come out to the left of **B**, at **C**.

2 Take the needle diagonally up to **D** and insert. Come out near the centre of the stitch at **E**.

3 Insert the needle at **F,** then bring it out to the left at **G**. Take it down at **H** to complete the cross.

······ TECHNIQUE VARIATION ·······

For a decorative effect, stitch the small cross in the centre of the star (see step 3) using a different coloured thread.

Woven Star

.... LEVEL ....
Intermediate

.... USES ....
*Powdered filling;
isolated stitch*

.... METHOD ....
*Five interwoven
straight stitches*

.... MATERIALS ....
Any fabric; any thread

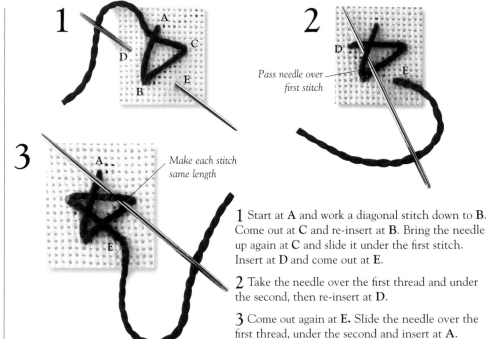

*Pass needle over
first stitch*

*Make each stitch
same length*

1 Start at **A** and work a diagonal stitch down to **B**. Come out at **C** and re-insert at **B**. Bring the needle up again at **C** and slide it under the first stitch. Insert at **D** and come out at **E**.

2 Take the needle over the first thread and under the second, then re-insert at **D**.

3 Come out again at **E.** Slide the needle over the first thread, under the second and insert at **A**.

Woven Cross

.... LEVEL ....
Intermediate

.... USES ....
*Powdered filling;
isolated stitch*

.... METHOD ....
*Four interwoven
straight stitches*

.... MATERIALS ....
*Any fabric;
any thick thread*

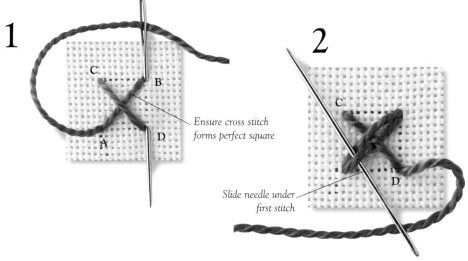

*Ensure cross stitch
forms perfect square*

*Slide needle under
first stitch*

1 Work a cross stitch (see p.50) from **A** to **B** and **C** to **D**. Bring the needle back up at **A**, insert it again at **B** and come out at **D**.

2 Pass the needle under the first thread and over the second, then insert at **C** to complete the cross.

French Knot

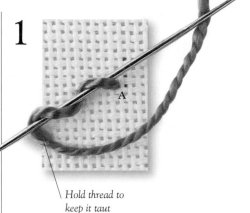

·········· LEVEL ··········
Intermediate

·········· USES ··········
Light or solid powdered filling; singly as raised highlight

········· METHOD ·········
Twisted knotted stitch

········· MATERIALS ·········
Any fabric; any thread depending on size; small-eyed needle

Hold thread to keep it taut

1 Start at **A**. Hold the thread taut and wrap it twice around the needle, then pull it gently to tighten the loops.

2 Maintaining the tension, insert the needle again at **A**, pushing it down through the two loops to form a round knot.

Take needle down at point where it emerged

········· STITCH VARIATION ·········

To work pistil stitch, insert the needle a short distance from where it emerged, to form a long tail. Make eight stitches in a circle to create a flower centre or floral shape.

Bullion Knot

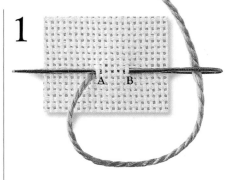

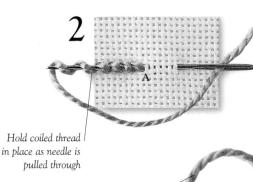

····· OTHER NAMES ·····
Caterpillar stitch

·········· LEVEL ··········
Intermediate

·········· USES ··········
Powdered filling; accent stitch; in rows as border

········· METHOD ·········
Long twisted knot

········· MATERIALS ·········
Any fabric; any twisted embroidery thread

Hold coiled thread in place as needle is pulled through

Pull thread up gently

1 Start at **A**. Take the needle down at **B** and bring the point back through at **A**.

2 Wrap the thread six times around the needle, holding the loops down with a finger. Using the other hand, pull the needle carefully through the fabric and the coiled thread.

3 Take the needle back down at **C** and pull the working thread up so that the loops lie flat.

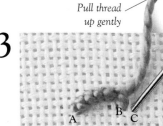

Danish Knot

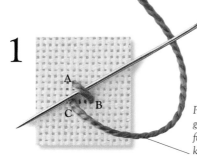

·········· LEVEL ··········
Intermediate

············ USES ············
*Powdered filling;
triangular accent stitch*

········· METHOD ·········
*Looped knot worked over
short diagonal stitch*

······· MATERIALS ·······
*Any fabric;
thick twisted thread*

*Pull loop up
gently to form
first part of
knot*

*Pull needle over
working thread*

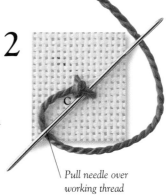

1 Start at **A** and work a short diagonal stitch down to **B**. Bring the needle out at **C** and slide it under the stitch from right to left.

2 Take the needle across to the right of the knot. Pass it under the diagonal stitch from right to left for a second time.

3 Insert the needle at **C** to complete the knot.

Four-legged Knot

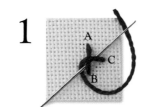

····· OTHER NAME ·····
Knot stitch

········· LEVEL ··········
Intermediate

············ USES ············
*Powdered filling;
isolated stitch*

······· METHOD ·······
*Upright cross with
knotted centre*

········· MATERIALS ·········
Any fabric; any thick thread

1 Start at **A** and work an upright stitch down to **B**. Come out at **C**. Loop the thread to the left, and slide the needle under the stitch.

2 Pull the thread gently to form a knot. Insert the needle at **D** to complete the stitch.

Sword

·········· LEVEL ··········
Easy

············ USES ············
*Worked randomly as light
filling; in rows as border*

········· METHOD ·········
Looped, elongated cross

····· MATERIALS ·····
*Any fabric; any
thick thread*

*Ensure B is
equidistant
from A and C*

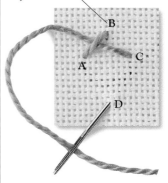

Start at **A** and work a loose diagonal stitch up to **B**. Bring the needle out at **C** and slide it under the stitch from right to left. Take it down at **D**, pulling gently so that the two stitches form a cross.

Fly

1

Pull needle over working thread

2

C
D

····· Other Names ·····
Y-stitch; open loop stitch

········· Level ·········
Easy

········· Uses ·········
Light or heavy filling; worked in horizontal or vertical rows as border

········ Method ········
Tied loop stitch

······· Materials ·······
Any fabric; any thick thread

1 Start at **A** and work a loose horizontal stitch across to **B**. Bring the needle out at **C**.

2 Take the needle down at **D** to make a tie stitch (see p.20).

Sheaf Filling

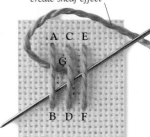

Pull stitches together to create sheaf effect

········· Level ··········
Intermediate

········· Uses ·········
Powdered filling; in rows as border; isolated stitch

········ Method ········
Three upright straight stitches tied at the centre

······· Materials ·······
Any fabric; any thick thread

Make three parallel straight stitches from **A** to **B**, **C** to **D** and **E** to **F**. Come up at **G** and pass the needle to the left, under the first stitch. Take the needle across to the right and slide it back under the stitches. Take it to the right again and pull the thread up gently. Insert at **G** to complete.

Crown

········· Level ·········
Intermediate

········· Uses ·········
Powdered filling; in rows as border; isolated stitch

········ Method ········
Looped stitch tied down with three straight stitches

······· Materials ·······
Any fabric; any thick thread

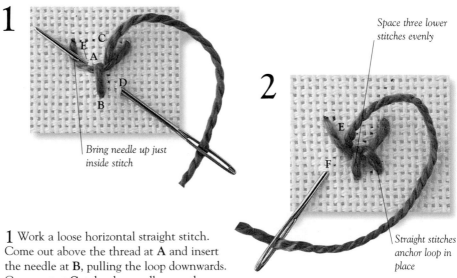

1

Bring needle up just inside stitch

2

Space three lower stitches evenly

Straight stitches anchor loop in place

1 Work a loose horizontal straight stitch. Come out above the thread at **A** and insert the needle at **B**, pulling the loop downwards. Come out at **C**, take the needle over the thread and insert at **D**, then come out at **E**.

2 Take the needle down over the thread and insert at **F** to complete the stitch.

Sorbello

·········· LEVEL ··········
Intermediate

·········· USES ··········
*In straight rows as filling;
in rows as border;
isolated stitch*

········ METHOD ········
Heavy square knot

······ MATERIALS ······
*Any fabric; twisted or
pearl threads give a
raised effect*

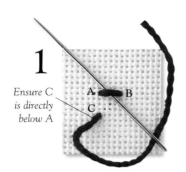

Ensure C is directly below A

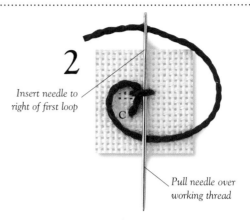

Insert needle to right of first loop

Pull needle over working thread

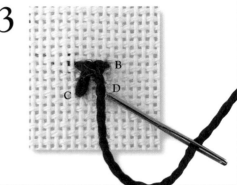

1 Start at **A** and work a short stitch to **B**. Bring the needle out below **A**, at **C**, and slide it under the stitch from bottom to top.

2 Hold the thread down to the left and pass the needle under the stitch again, this time from top to bottom.

3 Pull the thread gently to make a knot, then insert the needle below **B** at **D** to complete the stitch.

Palestrina Knot

·········· LEVEL ··········
Intermediate

·········· USES ··········
*Geometric filling;
worked in rows as border;
isolated stitch*

········ METHOD ········
Rectangular looped knot

······ MATERIALS ······
*Any fabric;
any thick thread*

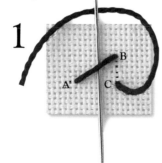

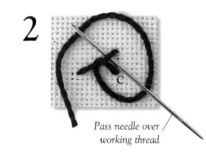

Pass needle over working thread

Ensure D is level with B and directly above A

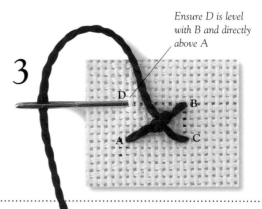

1 Start at **A** and work a diagonal stitch to **B**. Bring the needle out level with **A**, at **C**, and slide it under the stitch from top to bottom.

2 Pass the needle under the diagonal stitch again, from top to bottom and to the right of the first loop.

3 Pull the thread gently to form a knot, then take the needle down diagonally opposite **C**, at **D**, to complete the stitch.

Link

···· OTHER NAME ····
Detached chain stitch

···· LEVEL ····
Easy

···· USES ····
Scattered as light filling; leaves and flower petals

···· METHOD ····
Single looped stitch

···· MATERIALS ····
Any fabric; any thread

1

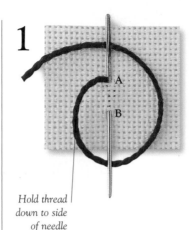

Hold thread down to side of needle

2

Tie stitch secures loop

1 Start at **A**. Make a loop and take the needle down at **A**. Come out at **B** and pull the needle through over the working thread.

2 Insert the needle directly below **B**, at **C**, making a tie stitch (see p.20) to complete.

···· STITCH VARIATION ····

Lazy daisy stitch is formed by making several link stitches in a circle, all starting at the centre. Each stitch represents a petal and the whole looks like a flowerhead.

Berry

···· LEVEL ····
Intermediate

···· USES ····
Powdered filling; flowers and leaves

···· METHOD ····
Double link stitch

···· MATERIALS ····
Any fabric; any thread

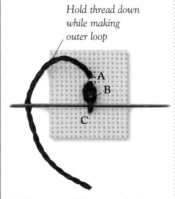

Hold thread down while making outer loop

Make a small link stitch (see above). Bring the needle out at **A** and slide it under the tie stitch between **B** and **C**. Take the needle back up and insert at **A** to complete the stitch.

Picot

···· OTHER NAME ····
Long-tailed daisy stitch

···· LEVEL ····
Easy

···· USES ····
Powdered filling; in circles as floral motif

···· METHOD ····
Link variation with long tie stitch

···· MATERIALS ····
Any fabric; any thread

Work elongated tie stitch to form tail

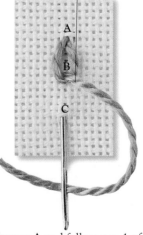

Start at **A** and follow step 1 of link stitch (see above). Take the needle down below **B**, at **C**, to make a long tie stitch.

Detached Wheatear

····· OTHER NAMES ·····
*Tete-de-boeuf stitch;
ox-head stitch*

········ LEVEL ·········
Intermediate

·········· USES ··········
*Powdered filling;
isolated stitch*

········ METHOD ········
*Link stitch worked over
loose straight stitch*

········ MATERIALS ·······
Any fabric; any thread

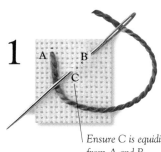

1

*Ensure C is equidistant
from A and B*

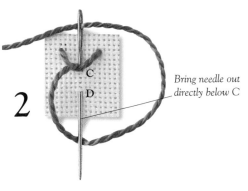

2

*Bring needle out
directly below C*

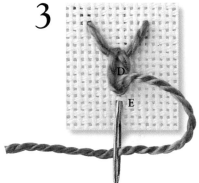

3

1 Start at **A**. Insert the needle at **B** and bring it out at **C**, passing over the working thread.

2 Make a loop and take the needle down at **C**. Come out at **D**, passing the needle over the working thread.

3 Take the needle down at **E** to form a short tie stitch (see p.20) to complete.

Tulip

········ LEVEL ·········
Intermediate

·········· USES ··········
*In alternate rows as
powdered filling;
naturalistic flowers*

········ METHOD ········
*Straight stitch worked
through link stitch*

········ MATERIALS ·······
Any fabric; any thread

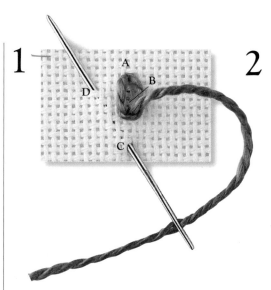

1

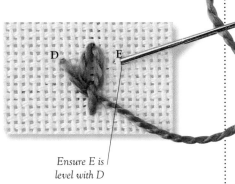

2

*Ensure E is
level with D*

1 Start at **A** and work a picot stitch (see p.80). Take the needle down at **C** and bring it out to the left, at **D**.

2 Pass the needle under the tie stitch and insert it at **E** to complete the 'leaves'.

········ TECHNIQUE VARIATION ·········

Make a slanting straight stitch on either side of the picot stitch, instead of a single one passing beneath the tie stitch (see step 2 above). This creates the effect of two separate leaves at the base of the flower.

Woven Spider Web

········· Level ·········
Intermediate

········· Uses ·········
Isolated stitch; large-scale powdered filling

········· Method ·········
Solid circle woven on foundation of seven straight stitches

········· Materials ·······
Any fabric; any thread in two colours; blunt needle

1

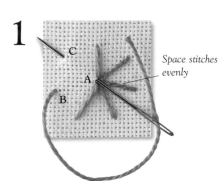

Space stitches evenly

2

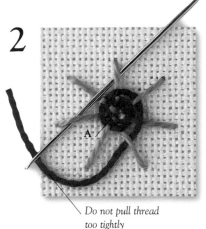

Do not pull thread too tightly

1 Work a foundation of five straight stitches (see p.73), all radiating from **A**. Bring the needle up at **B** and take it back down at **A**. Come out at **C**, ready to work the final stitch.

2 Bring the second thread up at **A**. Working clockwise, weave it alternately over and under the straight stitches until only the tips are left uncovered. Take the needle to the back to finish.

·········Stitch Variation·········

To make a ribbon rose, use a length of narrow silk embroidery ribbon for the weaving in step 2 (see above). Allow it to twist slightly to create the raised petal effect.

Ribbed Web

····· Other Name ·····
Ribbed spider web

········· Level ·········
Intermediate

········· Uses ·········
Isolated stitch

········· Method ·········
Back stitched spiral over large star stitch

········· Materials ·······
Any fabric; any thick thread in two colours; blunt needle

Work in anti-clockwise direction

Work a star stitch (see p.74) omitting the final cross. Come up at **A**. Slide the needle under the first two stitches to the left, then take it under the second and third stitches, making a back stitch (see p.40). Continue working round the star stitch until only the tips can be seen.

Buttonhole Wheel

Space stitches evenly around outer circle

········· Level ·········
Intermediate

········· Uses ·········
Isolated stitch

········· Method ·········
Buttonhole stitch worked within a ring

········· Materials ·······
Any fabric; any thread

Mark two concentric circles. Come up at **A**, and insert the needle at **B** on the inner circle. Bring the needle out at **C**, passing it over the working thread. Continue stitching until the ring is complete.

Shisha

.... LEVEL ....
Advanced

.... USES ....
Indian embroidery; with couched gold threads

.... METHOD ....
Mirror disc attached to fabric with ring of twisted stitches

.... MATERIALS ....
Any fabric; any thick thread; shisha mirror; frame

1
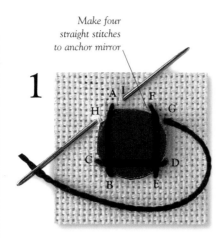
Make four straight stitches to anchor mirror

2
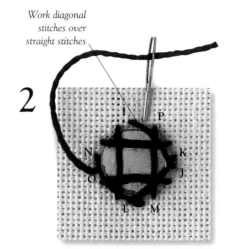
Work diagonal stitches over straight stitches

3
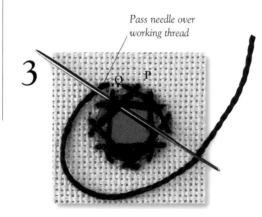
Pass needle over working thread

4
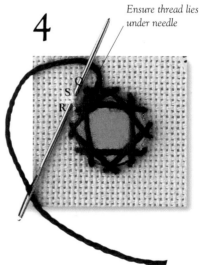
Ensure thread lies under needle

5
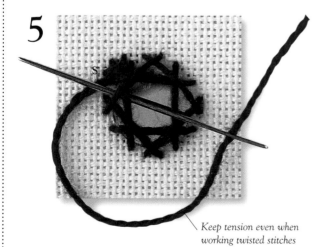
Keep tension even when working twisted stitches

1 Place the mirror in position. Start at **A** and work a straight stitch down to **B**. Come out at **C** and insert at **D**. Come up at **E** and down at **F**, then come out at **G** and go down at **H**. Bring the needle up at **I**, ready to start the next four stitches.

2 Take the needle down to **J** to make a diagonal stitch. Bring it out at **K** and insert at **L**. Come out at **M**, down at **N**, out at **O**, then take the needle up to **P** and insert.

3 Bring the needle out at **Q**, just outside the straight stitches and pass it beneath the threads from right to left.

4 Insert the needle at **R** and bring it up at **S**, to make a small back stitch. Pull it through over the working thread.

5 Slide the needle back under the straight stitches and pull it through gently over the looped thread. Repeat steps 4 and 5 all the way around the mirror to complete.

Open and Solid Filling Stitches

BOTH TYPES OF filling are stitched within a marked outline, which may be a curved naturalistic shape or a geometric block. Open fillings allow the background to show through, whereas solid fillings produce a densely stitched area and should be worked in a thick thread that covers the fabric completely. Some of these stitches have evolved as shading stitches, using several closely toning threads. With practice, these can produce subtle, three-dimensional effects, especially for flowers and foliage. The fabric should be mounted in a frame for all filling stitches.

Darning

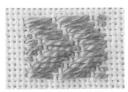

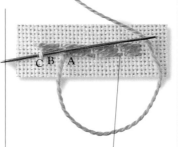

Work stitches so that spaces between them create a pattern

····· OTHER NAME ·····
Damask stitch

········ LEVEL ··········
Easy

········ USES ·········
Solid filling patterns; geometric bands

······· METHOD ·········
Closely spaced rows of running stitch

······ MATERIALS ·······
Evenweave fabric; any thread

Come up at **A**, to the right of the start of the stitch above. Insert the needle at **B**, to the right of the end of the stitch above. Bring the needle up one thread to the left, at **C**. Repeat, always following the previous line of stitching.

Double Darning

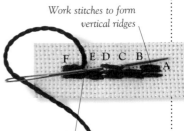

Work stitches to form vertical ridges

Ensure each row of stitches lines up with previous one

········ LEVEL ··········
Intermediate

········ USES ·········
Solid filling stitch that appears the same at front and back

······· METHOD ·········
Double running stitch in closely spaced rows

······ MATERIALS ·······
Evenweave fabric; any thread

Work a row of evenly spaced running stitches (see p.39), from **A** to **B**, **C** to **D** and **E** to **F**. Fill in the spaces on the return journey; bring the needle back out at **E**, insert at **D** and come out at **C**. Work the following rows directly above.

Brick and Cross

········ LEVEL ··········
Intermediate

··········· USES ···········
Open geometric filling

······· METHOD ·········
Alternate cross and groups of straight stitches, worked in vertical rows

······ MATERIALS ·······
Evenweave fabric; any thread

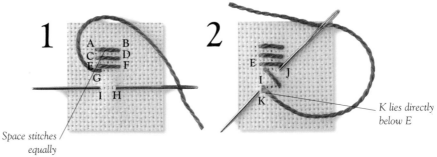

1 Space stitches equally

2 K lies directly below E

1 Make three parallel straight stitches from **A** to **B**, **C** to **D** and **E** to **F**. Bring the needle out at **G**. Work a diagonal stitch to **H**, then come out directly below **G**, at **I**.

2 Insert the needle at **J** to complete the cross stitch. Bring the needle out to the left of **I**, at **K**.

3 Insert at **L**, then make two more straight stitches. Come out level with **L**, at **M**, and insert at **N**. Bring the needle out at **O** and insert it at **P** to complete the second cross stitch. Come out at **Q** to begin the next three straight stitches.

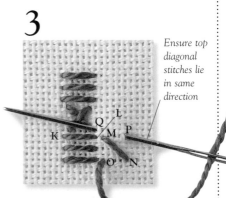

3 Ensure top diagonal stitches lie in same direction

Satin

····· OTHER NAME ·····
Damask stitch

········· LEVEL ··········
Intermediate

·········· USES ··········
Solid filling; bands

········ METHOD ········
Closely worked straight stitches

······· MATERIALS ·······
Any fabric; any thread – stranded silk or cotton gives lustrous finish

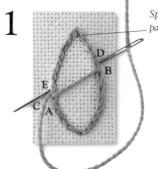

Split stitch creates padded edge

1 Outline the area to be covered with split stitch (see p.40). Start the satin stitch at the widest point of the shape. Work a diagonal stitch from **A** up to **B** and bring the needle out next to **A**, at **C**. Take it down next to **B**, at **D**. Come out at **E** ready for the next stitch.

2 Repeat, varying the stitch length until the top part of the shape is covered. Bring the needle out again just below **A** and work downwards to fill the rest of the shape.

Leave no space between stitches

Work each stitch at same angle

········· TECHNIQUE VARIATION ·········

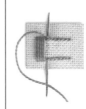

When working satin stitch over a geometric shape or as a border, work the stitches at a right angle to the outline. Start stitching at one end and work to the other.

Surface Satin

········· LEVEL ··········
Intermediate

·········· USES ··········
Solid filling; bands

········· METHOD ·········
Closely worked straight stitches: uses less thread than satin stitch

······· MATERIALS ·······
Any fabric; any thread – stranded silk or cotton for smooth surface; frame

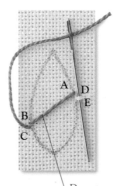

Do not make stitches too long

Mark the required shape. Work a diagonal stitch from **A** down to **B** and come up directly below, at **C**. Take the needle up to **D** and bring it out at **E**. Fill the lower part of the shape in this way. Come back up above **A** to work the remaining area.

Encroaching Satin

········· LEVEL ··········
Intermediate

·········· USES ··········
Solid filling for larger areas

········· METHOD ·········
Overlapping narrow rows of satin stitch

······· MATERIALS ·······
Any fabric; any thread, in shades of the same colour; frame

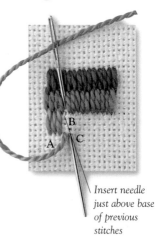

Insert needle just above base of previous stitches

Work a row of satin stitch (see above). On the following rows, bring the needle out at **A** and insert at **B**, between two stitches on the row above. Come up next to **A**, at **C**. Repeat to the row's end.

Long and Short

········ LEVEL ········
Advanced

········ USES ·········
*Shaded filling, giving
three-dimensional effect*

········ METHOD ·······
Interlocking satin stitches

········ MATERIALS ········
*Any fabric; any thread,
in shades of the same
colour; frame*

1

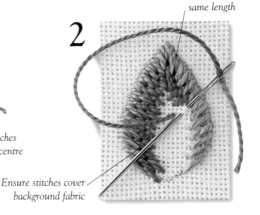

*Slant stitches
towards centre*

2

*Make stitches all
same length*

*Ensure stitches cover
background fabric*

1 Mark the outline of the area to be stitched. Work a row of alternate long and short satin stitches (see p.86) around the edge. Come up at **A** and take the needle down at **B** to make a long stitch. Bring it out at **C** to make a short stitch. Continue in this way to complete the first round.

2 Using a darker shade, work a row of long satin stitches which interlock with the first round. Fill in the centre with a third shade.

········ TECHNIQUE VARIATION ·········

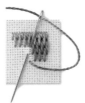

When filling square or rectangular shapes, work the first row in alternate long and short stitches and subsequent rows in long stitches only, so they interlock as before.

Buttonhole Filling

····· OTHER NAME ·····
Buttonhole shading

·········· LEVEL ·········
Intermediate

·········· USES ··········
Shaded filling

······· METHOD ········
*Overlapping rows of
buttonhole stitch*

····· MATERIALS ·····
*Any fabric; any thread,
in shades of the same
colour; frame*

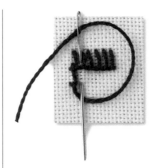

Work a row of buttonhole stitch (see p.58) using the lightest thread. With a darker tone, work the second row directly below, so that the upright stitches overlap the base of the previous row. Work subsequent rows in progressively darker tones to create the effect of shading.

Stem Filling

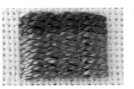

····· OTHER NAME ·····
Stem stitch shading

·········· LEVEL ··········
Intermediate

·········· USES ···········
Shaded filling

······· METHOD ········
*Closely spaced lines of
stem stitch*

····· MATERIALS ·····
*Any fabric; any thread, in
shades of the same colour*

Mark the outline of the area to be stitched. Using the darkest thread, work two rows of stem stitch (see p.41) along one side of the outline. Work the next two rows in a lighter shade. Continue to fill the shape with rows of stem stitch, graduating the colour to create a shaded effect.

Leaf

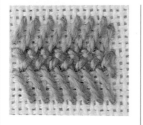

········· LEVEL ·········
Intermediate

········· USES ·········
*Open filling for leaves,
petals and wide borders*

········· METHOD ·········
*Overlapping diagonal
stitches worked upwards*

········· MATERIALS ·········
*Any fabric;
any thread; frame*

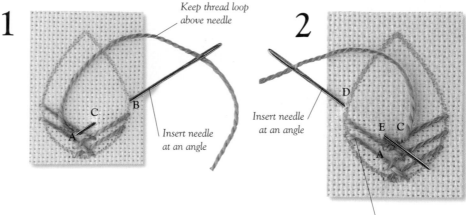

*Keep thread loop
above needle*

*Insert needle
at an angle*

*Insert needle
at an angle*

*Work pairs of
slanting stitches in
alternate directions*

1 Mark the required shape on the fabric. Come up at **A**, to the left of centre. Insert the needle at **B** and bring it through to the right of centre, at **C**.

2 Take the needle down at **D** and bring it up directly above **A**, at **E**. Repeat these two stitches to fill the space, decreasing the length as the leaf tapers to a point. Work a narrow outline stitch (see pp.38–46) around the outside edge to complete.

Open Fishbone

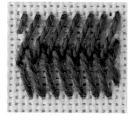

········· LEVEL ·········
Easy

········· USES ·········
*Light filling for small leaf or
petal shapes; open borders*

········· METHOD ·········
*Alternate slanting stitches,
worked downwards*

········· MATERIALS ·········
*Any fabric; any thread;
frame*

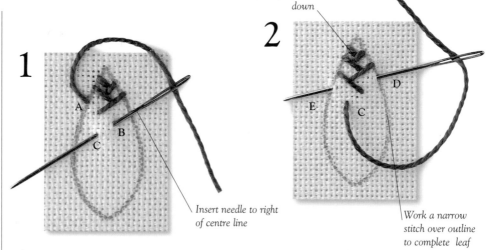

*Work stitches
alternately up and
down*

*Insert needle to right
of centre line*

*Work a narrow
stitch over outline
to complete leaf*

1 Mark the required shape. Come up at **A** and make a downwards slanting stitch to **B**, to the right of centre. Bring the needle out to the left of centre, at **C**.

2 Take the needle up to the right and insert at **D**. Come out at **E**, ready to work the next downwards stitch. Repeat these two stitches to continue, altering the length as the outline widens or narrows.

Attached Fly

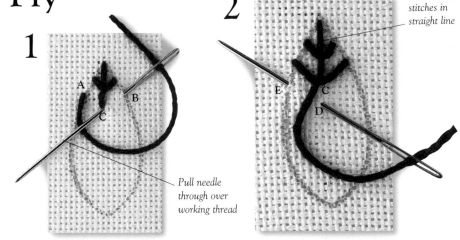

1

2

Work upright stitches in straight line

Pull needle through over working thread

····· OTHER NAME ·····
Fishbone

········ LEVEL ··········
Easy

·········· USES ··········
Open filling for narrow leaf or geometric shapes; light borders

········ METHOD ·········
Row of linked fly stitches worked downwards

····· MATERIALS ·······
Any fabric; any thread; embroidery frame

1 Mark the outline of the area to be filled. Come out at **A** and insert the needle on the same level, at **B**. Bring it up in the centre at **C**.

2 Insert the needle directly below **C**, at **D**, to make a straight stitch, and bring it out at **E**. Repeat steps 1 and 2 to continue, varying the stitch length as required.

········· STITCH VARIATION ·········

Close fly stitch is made by reducing the length of the straight stitches (see step 2).

Cretan

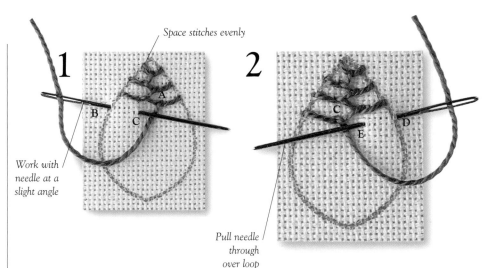

1

2

Space stitches evenly

Work with needle at a slight angle

Pull needle through over loop

····· OTHER NAME ·····
Cretan filling

········ LEVEL ··········
Easy

·········· USES ··········
Open filling for leaf or geometric motif; borders

········ METHOD ·········
Looped vertical stitch, worked downwards

····· MATERIALS ·······
Any fabric; any thread; frame

1 Mark the shape to be filled. Come up to the right of centre at **A**, then take the needle across to **B** and insert. Come out to the left of centre at **C**. Pull the needle through over the working thread.

2 Take the needle down at **D** and come out at **E**. Repeat these two steps to fill the required area.

·········· STITCH VARIATION··········

Close Cretan stitch is formed by working each new stitch immediately below the last, so no space is left between them.

Romanian Couching

········ LEVEL ········
Intermediate

········· USES ·········
Solid filling for large areas

······· METHOD ········
*Closely spaced long
couched stitches*

······ MATERIALS ·······
*Any fabric; any thread –
stranded cotton gives
smooth surface; frame*

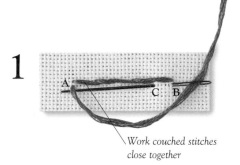

*Work couched stitches
close together*

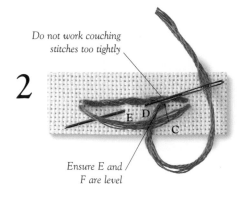

*Do not work couching
stitches too tightly*

*Ensure E and
F are level*

1 Come up at **A** and work a long horizontal stitch across to **B**. Bring the needle out level with **A**, at **C**.

2 Make a couching stitch: take the needle over the long stitch and insert at **D**. Draw the thread up gently to tighten. Come out at **E**, ready to make the next couching stitch.

········· STITCH VARIATION·········

Bokhara couching is worked in the same way, but the couching stitches are much shorter and made at a steep angle.

Spiral Couching

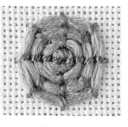

········ LEVEL ········
Intermediate

········· USES ·········
*Solid filling for circles;
metal thread embroidery*

······· METHOD ········
*Laid threads worked
within a circle*

······ MATERIALS ·······
*Any fabric; thick or
fragile threads; finer
couching thread; frame*

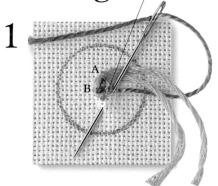

*Work first round of couching
stitches at right angles*

*Ensure laid
threads cover
fabric completely*

*Lay threads in a
clockwise spiral*

1 Mark a circle and bring the couching thread up just above the centre, at **A**. Fold the laid thread in half, pass the needle through the loop and insert at **B** to make a couching stitch. Curve the threads to the right. Work three more stitches, to complete the round. Make another round of four couching stitches.

2 Continue couching the laid threads in a spiral, spacing the stitches further apart as it increases in diameter. Take the ends through to the back to finish.

Couched Filling

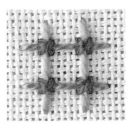

·········· LEVEL ··········
Intermediate

·········· USES ··········
Decorative open filling

·········· METHOD ··········
*Straight stitch grid with
cross stitch couching*

·········· MATERIALS ··········
*Any fabric; thread in
two colours of the same
or different
thicknesses; frame*

*Work upright stitches at right
angles to horizontal stitches*

*Ensure stitches
are parallel and
spaced evenly*

*Keep cross stitches small
for neat appearance*

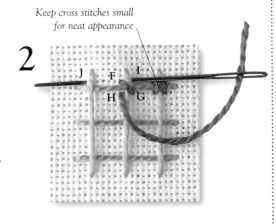

1 Using the first colour, make a foundation of horizontal straight stitches (see p.73). Come up at **A** to start working the vertical stitches. Take the needle down at **B**, then bring it out at **C**. Insert at **D** and come out at **E**, ready for the final stitch.

2 Work a cross stitch over each intersection of the straight stitches. Bring the second colour up at **F**. Take the needle down over the crossed threads and insert at **G**. Come up at **H** and insert at **I**, then come out at **J**, ready to make the next cross.

Laidwork

·········· LEVEL ··········
Advanced

·········· USES ··········
Decorative solid filling

·········· METHOD ··········
*Surface satin stitch with
trellis of couched straight
stitches*

·········· MATERIALS ··········
*Any fabric; thread in three
colours; frame*

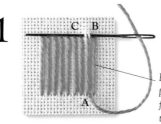

*Keep stitches
parallel so no
fabric shows
through*

*Ensure diagonal
stitches are
spaced evenly*

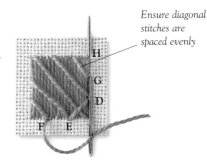

*Work tie stitches over
crossed threads*

1 Work a row of upright surface satin stitches (see p.86), leaving one stitch width between each. Bring the needle out at **A**, insert at **B** and come up at **C**. Repeat along the row to fill in the spaces.

2 Using the second thread, work a series of diagonal stitches across the foundation. Come up at **D** to start the second layer of stitches. Take the needle down at **E**, then bring it out at **F** and insert at **G**. Come out at **H**, ready to complete the trellis.

3 Work the short tie stitches (see p.20) in the third colour. Come up at **I**, take the needle down at **J** and bring it out again at **K**. Repeat at each intersection.

Back Stitch Trellis

········· LEVEL ·········
Intermediate

·········· USES ··········
Open geometric filling

········ METHOD ········
*Intersecting diagonal rows
of back stitch*

······· MATERIALS ·······
*Any fabric – evenweave
for a regular effect; any
embroidery thread*

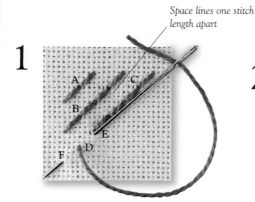

*Space lines one stitch
length apart*

1

*Work stitches into
holes made by
previous row*

2

*Stitch at right
angles to
previous row*

1 Work a series of diagonal, parallel rows of back stitch (see p.40). Start the first row at **A**, the second at **B** and the third at **C**. Come out at **D**, insert the needle at **E** and bring it out at **F**. Continue until the required area is filled.

2 Work the next row in the opposite direction, starting at **C**, then **G**. Come out at **H**, insert at **I** and come up at **J**. Repeat to complete the trellis.

Japanese Darning

········· LEVEL ·········
Intermediate

·········· USES ··········
*Open geometric filling
for larger areas*

········ METHOD ········
*Combination of running
and straight stitches*

······· MATERIALS ·······
*Any fabric – evenweave
is easier to use; any
embroidery thread*

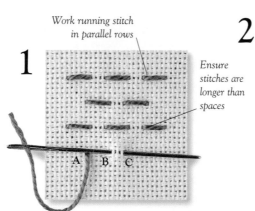

*Work running stitch
in parallel rows*

1

*Ensure
stitches are
longer than
spaces*

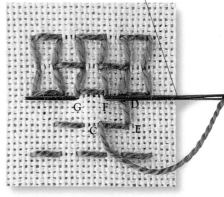

*Work slanting stitches
into holes made by
running stitches*

2

1 Work several horizontal rows of running stitch (see p.39), positioned so that the stitches in each row lie beneath the spaces in the row above. Come up at **A**, insert the needle at **B** and bring it out at **C**. Repeat to fill the required area.

2 Link the rows of running stitch with slanting stitches. Bring the needle out at **D** and take it down at **E**. Come up at **C**, go down at **F**, then up at **G**, ready to make the next stitch. Continue to the end of the row, before proceeding to the one below.

Cloud Filling

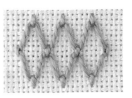

····· OTHER NAME ·····
Mexican stitch

········ LEVEL ········
Intermediate

········· USES ·········
Open filling; crewel work

······· METHOD ·······
*Interlaced rows of short
upright stitches*

····· MATERIALS ·····
*Any fabric – evenweave for
regular effect; any thread in
two colours; blunt needle*

1
*Position each
stitch between two
in row above*

B
C
A

Space stitches evenly

2
*Use blunt needle
for lacing*

D

3
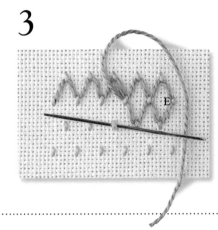
E

1 Work a foundation of short upright stitches, arranged in staggered rows. Come up at **A** and make a straight stitch to **B**, then bring the needle out at **C**. Repeat to fill the required area.

2 Bring the second thread up at **D**. Slide the needle under the first stitch in the top row from left to right. Pass it beneath the second stitch on the row below and continue lacing to the end.

3 Come up at **E**. Slide the needle under the first stitch on the third row, from right to left. Take it under the next stitch on the second row. Repeat to the end, then thread further rows in the same way.

Wave Filling

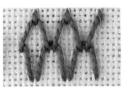

········ LEVEL ········
Intermediate

········· USES ·········
*Shaded or single colour
open filling; crewel work*

······· METHOD ·······
*Interlinked horizontal
rows of looped stitches*

····· MATERIALS ·····
*Any fabric; any thread in
one or more colours;
frame*

1
C B A

*Pick up a small amount
of fabric with needle*

2
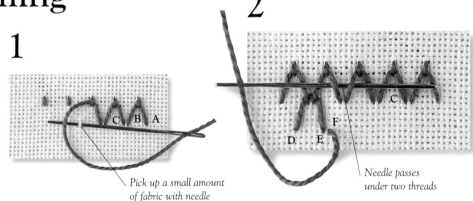
D E F C

*Needle passes
under two threads*

1 Work a base row of short, evenly spaced upright stitches. Come up at **A** and slide the needle under the first stitch. Take it back down to **B** and insert. Come out just to the left, at **C** and repeat to the end of the row.

2 Start the next row at **D**. Pass the needle under the next two stitches of the row above. Take it down and insert at **E**, then come out at **F**. Continue to the end of the row.

········ TECHNIQUE VARIATION ········

Create a subtly shaded effect by stitching each successive row in a darker shade of the same colour.

OPENWORK

PULLED FABRIC STITCHES

• • • • • • • ◆ • • • • • • •

DRAWN THREAD AND
INSERTION STITCHES

• • • • • • • ◆ • • • • • • •

CUTWORK AND
EDGING STITCHES

Pulled Fabric Stitches

Many of these stitches were originally worked as white-on-white stitches to decorate household linen, but their diversity and intricate patterns only really become apparent when coloured threads are used. They form all-over designs which vary in density; some are open and lacy, but others have a more solid pattern of stitches. Work on evenweave fabric which has been mounted in a frame. Avoid stretching the fabric too taut; it has to be fairly loose to allow the stitches to be worked evenly. Use strong thread in a weight to match the background fabric, and pull each stitch tightly to draw the fabric threads together.

Window Filling

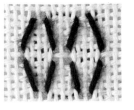

········ LEVEL ········

Level
Easy

Uses
Dense filling

Method
Diamond trellis with four small holes

Materials
Evenweave fabric; any thread; blunt needle; frame

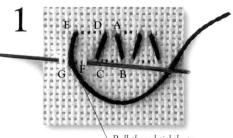

1

Pull thread tightly to create holes

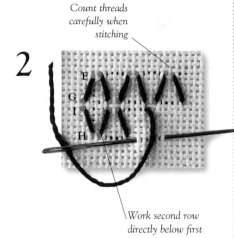

Count threads carefully when stitching

2

Work second row directly below first

1 Come up at **A**. Work a diagonal stitch over five horizontal and two vertical threads, down to **B**. Come out five threads to the left, at **C**, then insert one thread to the left of **A**, at **D**. Bring the needle out five threads to the left, at **E** and go down one thread to the left of **C**, at **F**. Come out at **G** and continue to the end of the row.

2 Stitch the next row as a mirror image of the first. Come up at **H**, eleven threads below **E**, and insert one thread below **G**, at **I**. Repeat these two rows to continue.

········ STITCH VARIATION ········

Pulled wave filling, which has open holes, is worked in the same way, but no space is left between the stitches.

Three-sided

Other Name
Straight line stitch

Level
Easy

Uses
Narrow borders

Method
Double back stitch worked in triangles

Materials
Evenweave fabric; any thread; blunt needle; frame

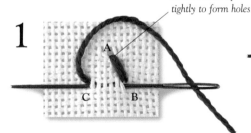

Draw thread up tightly to form holes

1

2

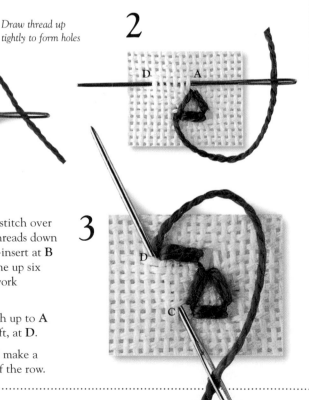

3

1 Start at **A** and work a diagonal stitch over six horizontal and three vertical threads down to **B**. Come out again at **A** and re-insert at **B** to make a double back stitch. Come up six threads to the left of **B** at **C** and work another double back stitch.

2 Work another double back stitch up to **A** and come out six threads to the left, at **D**.

3 Take the needle down to **C** and make a double stitch. Repeat to the end of the row.

Honeycomb Filling

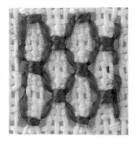

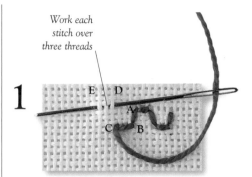

Work each stitch over three threads

1

Ensure stitches are all worked at right angles to each other

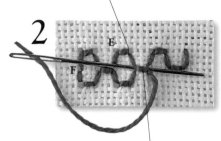

2

Make a double horizontal stitch at point where rows meet

········· LEVEL ·········
Intermediate

·········· USES ··········
Light filling with semi-open appearance

········· METHOD ·········
Worked to form hexagonal lattice

······· MATERIALS ·······
Evenweave fabric; any thread; blunt needle

1 Start at top right. Come up at **A**, go down at **B** and bring the needle out at **C**. Re-insert at **B** and come up again at **C**, then go down at **D**. Come up at **E**, re-insert the needle at **D**, and bring it out again at **E**. Repeat these four stitches to the end of the row.

2 Work the second row as a mirror image of the first. Start at **F**, and turn the work upside-down if desired. Repeat these two rows to fill the required area.

Russian Filling

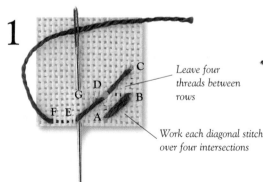

1

2

Leave four threads between rows

Work each diagonal stitch over four intersections

Pull stitches tightly to create large holes

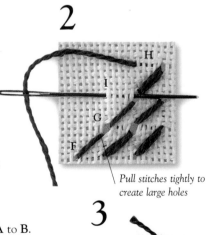

3

········· LEVEL ·········
Advanced

·········· USES ··········
Dense filling with open holes

········· METHOD ·········
Crossed diagonal stitches worked in two journeys

······· MATERIALS ·······
Evenweave fabric; any thread; blunt needle

1 Start at bottom right. Work a diagonal stitch from **A** to **B**. Come up at **C** and insert the needle at **D**. Bring it back up at **B**, down at **A**, then up again at **D** and down at **E**. Start the next row with a stitch from **F** to **G** and come up at **E**. Repeat these two rows until the top right corner of the area being filled is reached.

2 Work a stitch from **H** to **I** to square off the top edge, then continue working diagonal rows to fill the space.

3 The second journey, which completes the crosses, starts from **J** to **H**. Turn the work through 45 degrees to the left and stitch as before.

Diagonal Raised Band

········ LEVEL ········
Easy

·········· USES ··········
Ridged diagonal borders

······· METHOD ·······
*Diagonal row of tightly
worked cross stitches*

······ MATERIALS ······
*Evenweave fabric; any
thread; blunt needle;
frame*

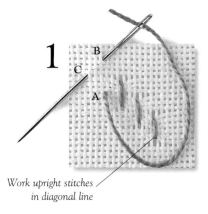

*Work upright stitches
in diagonal line*

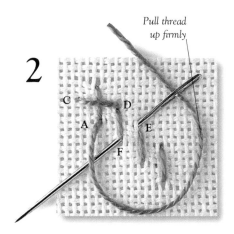

*Pull thread
up firmly*

1 Work a row of upright stitches. Come out at
A, take the needle up over six threads and insert
it at **B**. Bring the needle out three intersections
to the left, at **C**.

2 Insert the needle at **D** and bring it out again
at **A**. Insert at **E** and come out at **F**, and
continue to the end of the row.

········ STITCH VARIATION ········

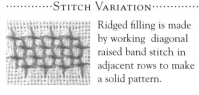

Ridged filling is made
by working diagonal
raised band stitch in
adjacent rows to make
a solid pattern.

Punch

········ LEVEL ········
Easy

·········· USES ··········
*Open filling with large
holes*

······· METHOD ·······
*Double back stitch worked
in square grid*

······ MATERIALS ······
*Evenweave fabric; any
thread; blunt needle;
frame*

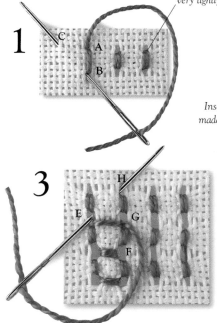

*Work double stitches
very tightly*

*Insert needle into hole
made by previous stitch*

1 Come up at **A** and work an upright stitch over
four threads to **B**. Make a second stitch in the
same holes, then come out five intersections to
the left, at **C**. Repeat to the end of the row.

2 Bring the needle out five threads below the
final stitch, at **D**. Work a double back stitch
between **D** and **E**, then come up five threads to
the right, at **F**. Continue to the end of the row
then repeat to fill the required area.

3 Work horizontal stitches between the upright
rows. Come up at **G** and make a double back
stitch to **E**. Bring the needle out at **H**, then
continue working up and down the rows.

Cobbler Filling

·········· LEVEL ··········
Intermediate

·········· USES ··········
Light, open filling

········· METHOD ·········
*Straight stitches worked in
vertical and horizontal
rows to form pattern of
detached squares*

······· MATERIALS ·······
*Evenweave fabric; any
thread; blunt needle; frame*

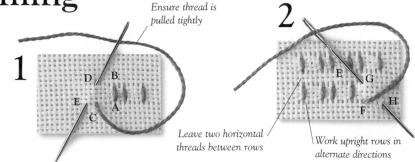

*Ensure thread is
pulled tightly*

*Leave two horizontal
threads between rows*

*Work upright rows in
alternate directions*

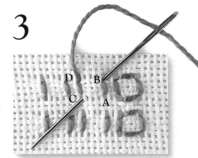

1 Come up at **A** and take the needle up over four threads to **B**. Bring it out four threads to the left of **A** at **C**. Insert at **D** and come up two threads to the left of **C** at **E**. Repeat to the end of the row.

2 Work the following rows of upright stitches in line with the first. Bring the needle up six threads below the previous stitch, at **F**. Insert at **G** and come up at **H**.

3 Join the pairs of stitches to form squares. Bring the needle up at **D**, take it down at **B** and up at **C**. Insert at **A**, then continue working down and up the rows.

Step

·········· LEVEL ··········
Intermediate

·········· USES ··········
Dense filling

········· METHOD ·········
*Diagonal rows made up
of blocks of satin stitch
set at alternate angles*

······· MATERIALS ·······
*Evenweave fabric;
any thread; blunt
needle; frame*

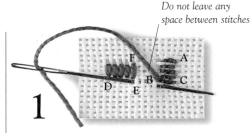

*Do not leave any
space between stitches*

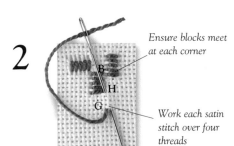

*Ensure blocks meet
at each corner*

*Work each satin
stitch over four
threads*

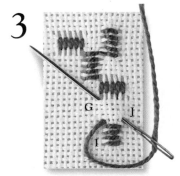

1 Start at **A**. Work a block of five horizontal stitches over four threads, ending with **B** to **C**. Come up eight threads to the left of **B**, at **D**. Work five upright stitches over four threads, ending with **E** to **F**. Come out at **B**, insert at **E** and work four more horizontal stitches.

2 Come up eight threads below **B**, at **G**. Insert at **H**, work four more upright satin stitches.

3 Bring the needle out eight threads below **G**, at **I**. Work five stitches over four threads, ending at **J**. Come up at **G** to make a block of upright stitches. Continue making alternate blocks to fill the required area.

Mosaic Filling

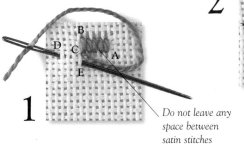

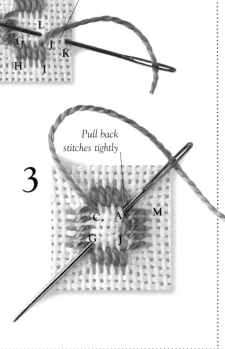

Ensure all satin stitches are worked over four threads

Do not leave any space between satin stitches

Pull back stitches tightly

········· LEVEL ·········
Advanced

·········· USES ··········
Dense chequered filling

········ METHOD ········
Block of satin stitch set in a square with back stitch centre

······ MATERIALS ······
Evenweave fabric; any thread; blunt needle; frame

1 Start at **A**. Work five satin stitches (see p.86) over four threads, finishing at **B**. Come out at **C**. Insert four threads to the left, at **D**, and come out at **E**.

2 Work four more horizontal stitches, finishing at **F**. Come up at **G** and insert the needle four threads below, at **H**. Work four more upright stitches, ending at **I**. Come up at **J**, insert at **K** and come out at **L**.

3 Work four more stitches, ending at **M**. Come back up at **A** and insert at **J**. Work three more back stitches from **C** to **A**, **G** to **C** and **J** to **G** to complete. Start the next stitch to the left (see Gallery p.31).

Diagonal Satin Filling

Leave five vertical threads between rows

Pull stitches tightly to create diamond

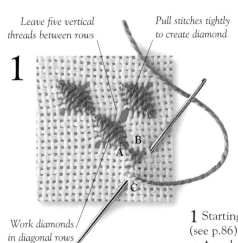

Work diamonds in diagonal rows

Stitch into holes made by previous blocks

········· LEVEL ·········
Intermediate

·········· USES ··········
Dense geometric filling

········ METHOD ········
Diagonal rows of satin stitch diamonds, worked in alternate directions

······ MATERIALS ······
Evenweave fabric; any thread; blunt needle; frame

1 Starting at top right, work a series of satin stitch (see p.86) diamonds to fill the required area. Come up at **A** and make a diagonal stitch over one intersection to **B**. Work four more stitches, increasing the length of each by one thread. Come up at **C** to work the longest stitch, then complete the diamond with four stitches which decrease in size.

2 Fill in the spaces with further rows of diamonds worked in the same way but in the opposite direction.

Back Stitch Rings

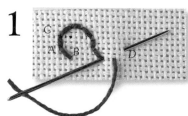

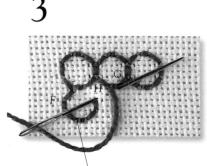

Stitch return journey in opposite direction

Work each back stitch over two vertical threads

········ **LEVEL** ········
Intermediate

········ **USES** ···········
Filling for large areas

······· **METHOD** ········
Intersecting rows of back stitch forming pattern of small circles

······ **MATERIALS** ·······
Evenweave fabric; any thread; blunt needle; frame

1 Start at **A** and take the needle down over two intersections, at **B**. Come up two threads above **A**, at **C**, then continue working alternate straight and diagonal back stitches to form a row of semi-circles.

2 Work a full circle at the end of the row. The lines cross at the upright stitches; work a second back stitch between **E** and **D**, then continue stitching from right to left.

3 Come up at **F** to start the next row. Work from left to right, making a second horizontal stitch between **G** and **H**, and at each point where two rows meet.

Algerian Eye

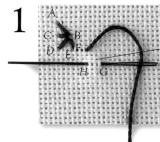

Work stitches over three vertical threads

Pull stitches tightly to create centre holes

········ **LEVEL** ·········
Intermediate

········ **USES** ···········
Chequerboard filling for large areas

········ **METHOD** ·········
Straight stitch stars worked in two journeys

······ **MATERIALS** ·······
Evenweave fabric; any thread; blunt needle; frame

1 Start at **A** and take the needle down over three intersections, at **B**. Come up three threads to the left, at **C** and insert at **B**. Bring the needle up at **D**, down at **B**, up at **E** and down at **B**. Come out three threads to the right of **E**, at **F**. For the next half star, go down over three intersections, at **G**, and up at **H**.

2 Continue stitching downwards, working half stars to fill the required area. Complete the final star with four more straight stitches, finishing at **I**. Insert at **G** to continue the second journey.

3 Come up at **J**, six threads to the right of the top star, ready to work the next diagonal row of stars.

Outlined Diamond Eyelet

·········· LEVEL ··········
Advanced

·········· USES ··········
Dense filling

········ METHOD ········
*Straight stitch diamond
worked into centre hole
with satin stitch border*

······ MATERIALS ······
*Evenweave fabric; any
thread; blunt needle;
frame*

1

*Pull thread tightly
to form eyelet*

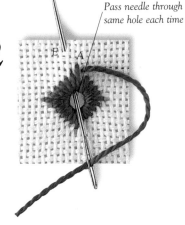

2

*Pass needle through
same hole each time*

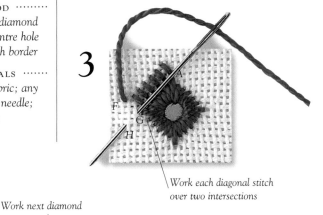

3

*Work each diagonal stitch
over two intersections*

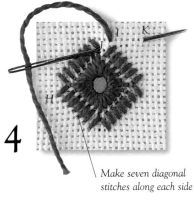

4

*Make seven diagonal
stitches along each side*

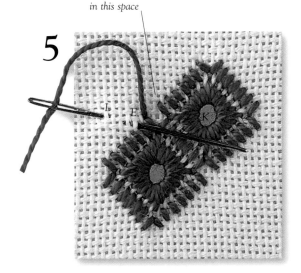

5

*Work next diamond
in this space*

1 Start at **A** and take the needle down over six threads to **B**. Come up one intersection to the left of **A** and insert at **B**, then make four more clockwise diagonal stitches, ending with **C** to **B**. Come up at **D**, and work the remaining three quarters of the diamond in the same way.

2 When the diamond is complete, bring the needle up two intersections to the left of **A**, at **E**.

3 Insert the needle at **A**, then make a further six parallel straight stitches, ending with **F** to **G**. Come out two intersections down to the left, at **H**. Work similar rows of straight stitch along the other three sides.

4 Make the final stitch from **I** to **J**. Come up six threads to the right, at **K**, and repeat steps 1 to 3 to work the next diamond.

5 To work the next diamond to the left, come back up at **E** and take the needle down six threads to the left, at **L**.

Drawn Thread and Insertion Stitches

DRAWN THREAD HEM and border stitches developed as a method of producing a decorative neatened edge on a piece of fabric. They should be worked on evenweave fabric from which a band of threads has been withdrawn. The remaining threads are then bunched together with tighly pulled stitches to form a regular pattern. Insertion stitches, also known as faggoting, have developed from old seaming techniques into a group of intricate stitches, which can be worked on plain or evenweave fabric. The two edges being joined must be mounted on paper so that the stitches can be spaced evenly.

Single Hem

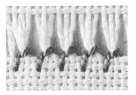

········· LEVEL ·········
Easy

········· USES ·········
Simple open border for hemmed edge

········ METHOD ········
Small groups of threads pulled into clusters along hem; worked on wrong side of fabric

······ MATERIALS ······
Evenweave fabric; any thread; blunt needle

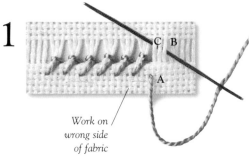

Work on wrong side of fabric

1

2

Pull thread tightly to bunch threads

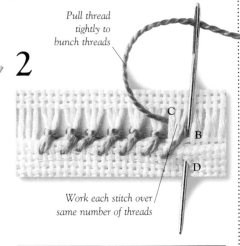

Work each stitch over same number of threads

1 Draw out a few threads along the edge of the fabric (see p.21). Fold a double hem to the base of the threads and tack down. Come up at **A** and slide the needle under three threads to the right, from **B** to **C**.

2 Take the needle down at **B** and bring it out at **D**. Repeat these two steps to continue.

········· STITCH VARIATION ·········

Ladder hem stitch is worked over a wider band of drawn threads. Work as for single hem stitch, then turn the fabric upside down and work a second row over the same groups of threads, making a series of bars.

Serpentine Hem

····· OTHER NAME ·····
Trellis hem stitch

····· LEVEL ·····
Easy

····· USES ·····
Decorative edging

······ METHOD ······
Two staggered rows of hem stitch worked to create slanting bars

····· MATERIALS ·····
Evenweave fabric; any thread; blunt needle

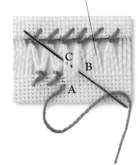

Withdraw several threads to create wide band

Work a row of hem stitch over groups of four threads (see above), then turn the fabric upside down. Come up at **A**. Pass the needle under two threads from each group, from **B** to **C**, and work a second row of hem stitch.

Antique Hem

····· LEVEL ·····
Easy

····· USES ·····
Plain border for hem

······ METHOD ······
Hem stitch variation in which horizontal stitches only show on right side

······ MATERIALS ······
Evenweave fabric; any thread; blunt needle

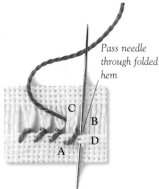

Pass needle through folded hem

Prepare the fabric as for single hem stitch (see above). With the wrong side facing, come up at **A**. Slide the needle under three threads to the right, from **B** to **C**. Insert the needle through the edge of the fold at **B** and come out at **D**. Pull up the thread; repeat this step to continue.

Italian Border

····· OTHER NAME ·····
Italian hem stitch

·········· LEVEL ··········
Easy

··········· USES ···········
*Open band; with hem
stitch as decorative border*

········· METHOD ·········
*Open border stitch,
worked in two journeys*

······· MATERIALS ·······
*Evenweave fabric; any
thread; blunt needle*

*Draw up loop to
pull threads together*

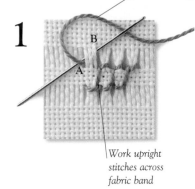

*Work upright
stitches across
fabric band*

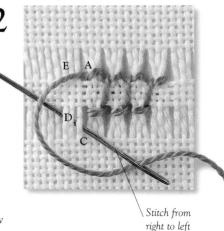

*Stitch from
right to left*

1 Withdraw two bands of threads leaving a narrow centre strip of fabric (see p.21). Come out at **A**. Take the needle across three threads to the right and then slide it behind the fabric from **B** to **A**.

2 Take the needle down to **C**. Slide it behind three threads and come out at **D**. Go back down at **C** and come up at **E**, three threads to the left of **A**. Repeat steps 1 and 2 to continue.

Four-sided

········· LEVEL ·········
Intermediate

··········· USES ···········
*Open bands; can also
be worked as pulled
fabric stitch*

········· METHOD ·········
*Pulled straight stitches,
worked horizontally to
form square pattern*

······· MATERIALS ·······
*Evenweave fabric; any
thread; blunt needle*

*Work over same
threads at top
and bottom*

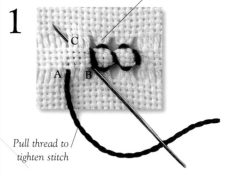

*Pull thread to
tighten stitch*

*Insert needle
alternately from
left to right*

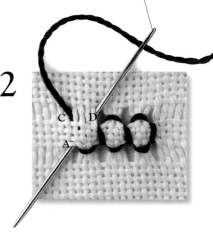

1 Withdraw two bands of threads leaving a narrow strip of fabric between them (see p.21). Come up at **A**. Take the needle down four threads to the right, at **B**. Bring it out directly above **A**, at **C**.

2 Take the needle down four threads to the right, at **D** and come up at **A**. Go down at **C** to make a vertical stitch and come up four threads to the left of **A**, ready to start the next stitch. Repeat these two steps to continue.

Chevron Border

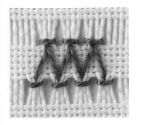

········ LEVEL ·········
Intermediate

·········· USES ············
*Decorative open bands;
with hem stitch as edging*

········ METHOD ·········
*Chevron stitch variation;
worked horizontally*

······ MATERIALS ·······
*Evenweave fabric; any
thread; blunt needle*

*Pull through over
working thread*

1

C D
B
A

*Draw horizontal
stitches up firmly*

2

B

E G
F

*Do not pull diagonal
stitches tightly*

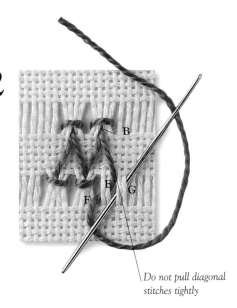

1 Prepare the fabric as for step 1 below. Come up at **A**. Take the needle diagonally up and slide it behind two threads from **B** to **C**. Take the needle across four threads to the right, and insert at **D**. Come up again at **B**.

2 Insert the needle at **E**. Slide it behind two threads to the left and come up at **F**. Take the needle across four threads and insert at **G**. Bring it out at **E** and pull through over the working thread. Repeat these two steps to the end of the row.

Diamond Border

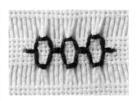

········ LEVEL ·········
Intermediate

·········· USES ············
*Open border with
hexagonal pattern*

········ METHOD ·········
*Pulled straight stitches,
worked in two journeys*

······ MATERIALS ·······
*Evenweave fabric; any
thread; blunt needle*

1

D C
A B

*Work each
horizontal stitch
over same number
of threads*

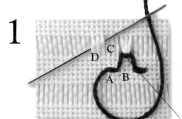

2

D C
F E

*Pull horizontal
stitches tightly*

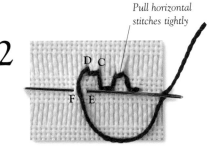

1 Withdraw two bands of thread leaving a narrow strip of fabric between them (see p.21). Come up in the centre, at **A**. Take the needle down three threads to the right, at **B**, then bring it out at **A** again. Insert directly above, at **C** and slide the needle under three threads to the left, coming up at **D**.

2 Take the needle down at **C** and come back up at **D**. Insert it directly below, at **E** and come out on the same level, at **F**. Repeat steps 1 and 2 to the end of the row.

3 Turn the fabric the other way up to work the second journey. Come up at **G** and stitch as before.

*Work second
journey as
mirror image
of first*

3

G

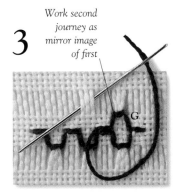

Laced Insertion

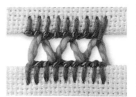

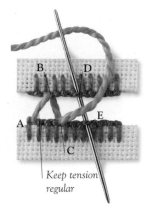

Keep tension regular

····· Other Name ·····
Laced faggot stitch

········ Level ·········
Easy

·········· Uses ··········
Decorative joining stitch

········ Method ·········
Two hems worked with Antwerp edging stitch, linked with interlacing

········ Materials ········
Evenweave fabric; thick thread; blunt needle

Mount the fabric (see p.21). Work a row of Antwerp edging stitch (see p.112) along each hem. Come up at **A**. Pass the needle down over **B**. Slide it under **C**, from back to front. Take it over **D**, from front to back; repeat to the end of the seam.

Cretan Insertion

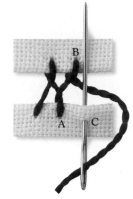

········· Level ·········
Easy

·········· Uses ··········
Simple join for two straight edges

········ Method ·········
Open Cretan stitch adapted as insertion

········ Materials ········
Evenweave fabric; thick thread; blunt needle

Mount the fabric on paper (see p.21). Take the needle through to the back at **A**, then insert it from the front at **B**. Bring it through behind the diagonal thread and take it down at **C**. Pull through over the working thread. Repeat to the end of the seam.

Faggot Bundles

········ Level ·········
Intermediate

·········· Uses ··········
Decorative method of joining two edges

········ Method ·········
Groups of two stitches bound by a third, worked from top to bottom

········ Materials ········
Evenweave fabric; any thread; blunt needle

Loop thread from left to right

Pull thread tightly to bunch stitches

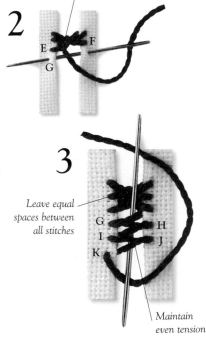

Leave equal spaces between all stitches

Maintain even tension

1 Mount the fabric (see p.21). Start on the left, at **A** and work a straight stitch across to **B**, on the right. Make another stitch from **C** to **D**, then come out at **E**. Pass the needle behind all the threads, then pull through over the loop.

2 Insert the needle at **F**, then bring it out below **E** at **G**, ready to start the next group of stitches.

3 Insert at **H**, then make another stitch from **I** to **J**. Come out at **K**, take the needle behind the three diagonal and two horizontal threads, and pull through over the working thread. Repeat steps 1 to 3 to continue.

Knotted Insertion

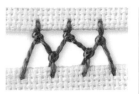

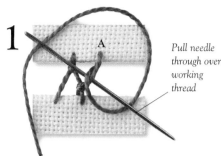

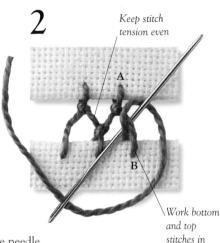

Pull needle through over working thread

Keep stitch tension even

Work bottom and top stitches in same way

····· OTHER NAME ·····
Knotted faggot stitch

········· LEVEL ··········
Advanced

·········· USES ··········
Decorative method of joining two edges

········· METHOD ·········
Knotted joining stitch worked horizontally

········· MATERIALS ·········
Evenweave fabric; thick thread; blunt needle

1 Mount the fabric on paper (see p.21). Take the needle down through the top hem at **A** and bring it out to the left of the diagonal stitch. Loop the working thread to the right and pass the needle under both threads. Pull the thread up tightly to form a knot.

2 Take the needle down to the bottom hem and insert at **B**. Bring it through to the left of the diagonal stitch and loop the thread to the right. Slide the needle under both threads and pull through tightly. Continue stitching alternately up and down to the end of the seam.

Buttonhole Insertion

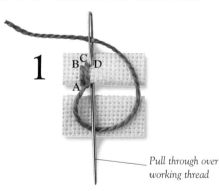

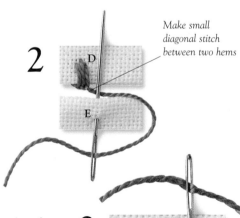

Pull through over working thread

Make small diagonal stitch between two hems

Work longest stitch in centre

····· OTHER NAME ·····
Buttonhole faggot stitch

········· LEVEL ··········
Advanced

·········· USES ··········
Decorative joining method

········· METHOD ·········
Groups of three buttonhole stitches worked alternately from top to bottom

········· MATERIALS ·········
Evenweave fabric; thick thread; blunt needle

1 Mount the fabric on paper (see p.21). Start at **A** and work a buttonhole stitch (see p.58) up to **B**. Work a second, longer stitch to **C**, then come out on the same level as **B**, at **D**, to work the third stitch.

2 Take the needle down through the bottom hem, at **E** and pull it through over the working thread.

3 Work two more buttonhole stitches at **F** and **G**, varying the length as before, then take the needle back up to the top hem at **H**. Make two more stitches at **I** and **J**, then continue to the end of the seam.

Needleweaving Bars

Work each bar over even number of threads

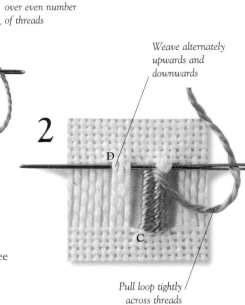

Weave alternately upwards and downwards

Pull loop tightly across threads

······· Other Name ·······
Woven bars

······· LEVEL ·······
Advanced

······· USES ·······
Flat, heavy borders

······· METHOD ·······
Weaving stitch, worked horizontally

······· MATERIALS ·······
Evenweave fabric; any thread; blunt needle

1 Withdraw a band of threads from the fabric. (see p.21). Come up at **A** and take the needle across three threads to the right. Insert it at **B** and bring it back through at **A**. Insert over three threads to the left at **C**, then come back out in the centre, at **A**. Continue weaving upwards.

2 When the bar is complete, bring the needle out three threads to the left, at **D**. Work downwards as before, then continue weaving bars to the end of the row.

Zigzag Clusters

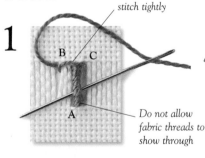

Pull double stitch tightly

Do not allow fabric threads to show through

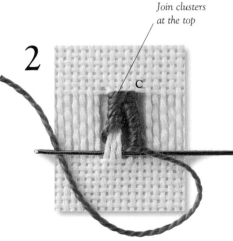

Join clusters at the top

······· LEVEL ·······
Advanced

······· USES ·······
Heavy open borders

······· METHOD ·······
Round, wrapped bars worked over foundation of drawn threads

······· MATERIALS ·······
Evenweave fabric; any thread; blunt needle

1 Withdraw a band of threads (see p.21). Start at **A** and take the needle over three threads to the right. Come back up at **A**, then pass the needle in front of and behind the threads. Continue wrapping to the top, then come out three threads to the left, at **B**. Take the needle across six threads and insert at **C**, then come back up at **B**. Insert again at **C** and come up between the two groups of threads.

2 Take the needle back over three threads and continue wrapping to the bottom. Start the next and subsequent clusters three threads to the left.

······· STITCH VARIATION ·······

Corded clusters are worked in the same way, but without the double linking stitches.

Cutwork and Edging Stitches

EDGING STITCHES GIVE an ornamental finish to a hem, and look particularly effective when worked in a thick, twisted thread. The stitches should be spaced regularly, but they can be worked on evenweave or plainweave fabric. Cutwork stitches, like the other types of openwork, were grouped under the name of 'white work'. Eyelets in various shapes can be used to decorate collars, mats and garments or combined with satin stitch to create *Broderie Anglaise* designs on lawn. Work these stitches on fine plainweave cotton or linen, in white or coloured threads, with or without a frame.

Antwerp Edging

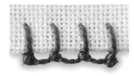

····· OTHER NAME ·····
Knotted blanket stitch

········· LEVEL ··········
Intermediate

··········· USES ············
Decorative hems

······· METHOD ········
*Blanket stitch variation,
worked horizontally over
edge of fabric*

······· MATERIALS ·······
*Any fabric; thick twisted
threads give best
stitch definition*

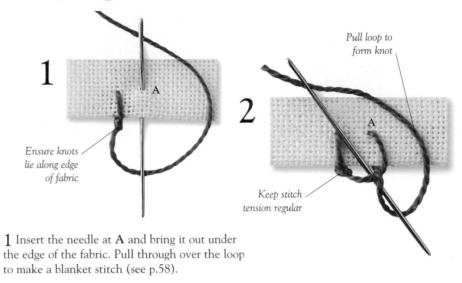

*Ensure knots
lie along edge
of fabric*

*Pull loop to
form knot*

*Keep stitch
tension regular*

1 Insert the needle at **A** and bring it out under the edge of the fabric. Pull through over the loop to make a blanket stitch (see p.58).

2 Take the needle back to the left and pass it behind the two threads. Draw up the working thread to form a knot. Repeat these two steps to continue along the edge.

Sailor Edging

········· LEVEL ··········
Intermediate

··········· USES ············
Decorative hems

········· METHOD ·········
*Blanket stitch variation,
worked downwards over
edge of fabric*

······· MATERIALS ·······
*Any fabric; any twisted
thread*

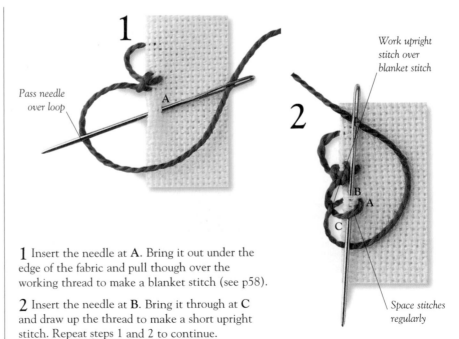

*Pass needle
over loop*

*Work upright
stitch over
blanket stitch*

*Space stitches
regularly*

1 Insert the needle at **A**. Bring it out under the edge of the fabric and pull though over the working thread to make a blanket stitch (see p58).

2 Insert the needle at **B**. Bring it through at **C** and draw up the thread to make a short upright stitch. Repeat steps 1 and 2 to continue.

Looped Edge

········· LEVEL ·········
Intermediate

·········· USES ··········
*Solid stitch for hems and
neatening raw edges;
foundation for laced
insertion stitch*

········· METHOD ·········
*Looped edging stitch,
worked horizontally*

······ MATERIALS ······
*Any fabric; any thread
depending on fabric*

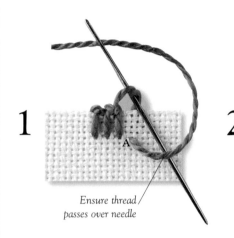

Work stitches closely together to conceal edge

Ensure thread passes over needle

Keep stitches same length

1 Come up at **A**. Take the needle to the left and pass it downwards through the loop. Pull up the thread gently.

2 Bring the needle out at **B**, ready to make the next stitch. Repeat these two steps to continue.

Half Chevron

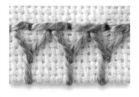

········· LEVEL ·········
Intermediate

·········· USES ··········
*To neaten folded edges
and hems*

········· METHOD ·········
*Chevron stitch variation,
worked over edge of fabric*

······ MATERIALS ······
Any fabric; any thread

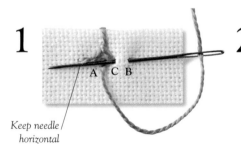

Keep needle horizontal

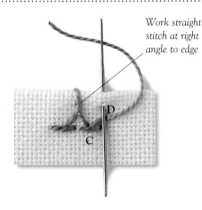

Work straight stitch at right angle to edge

1 Come up at **A**, insert the needle at **B** and bring it out in the centre, at **C**.

2 Loop the thread from left to right. Take the needle behind the fabric and bring it through over the working thread, at **D**.

3 Insert the needle to the right of **B**, at **E**, then bring it through again at **B**. Repeat steps 1 to 3 to continue along the edge.

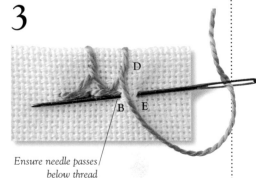

Ensure needle passes below thread

Scalloped Edge

·········· LEVEL ··········
Intermediate

·········· USES ··········
*Neatening curved and
scalloped raw edges*

········· METHOD ·········
*Buttonhole stitch worked
over running stitch
foundation*

······· MATERIALS ·······
*Closely woven fabric; any
fine thread; embroidery
scissors*

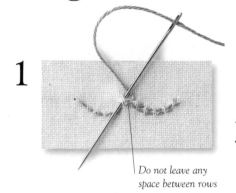

1

*Do not leave any
space between rows*

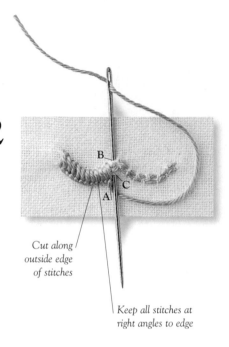

2

*Cut along
outside edge
of stitches*

*Keep all stitches at
right angles to edge*

1 Sew two foundation rows of closely spaced running stitch (see p.39) along the outline of the edge to be worked.

2 Work a row of buttonhole stitch (see p.58) over the foundation, following the curve of the outline. Come up at **A**, insert at **B** and pull the needle through at **C**. Repeat to the end of the line. When the stitching is complete, trim away the surplus fabric using sharp embroidery scissors.

Ring Picot Edge

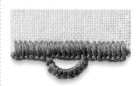

·········· LEVEL ··········
Advanced

·········· USES ··········
*Decorative trim on
buttonholed edges*

········· METHOD ·········
*Buttonhole stitch worked
over thread loop*

······· MATERIALS ·······
*Closely woven fabric, any
fine thread; embroidery
scissors*

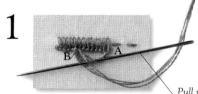

1

*Pull needle
through to make
buttonhole stitch*

*Do not pull stitches
too tightly*

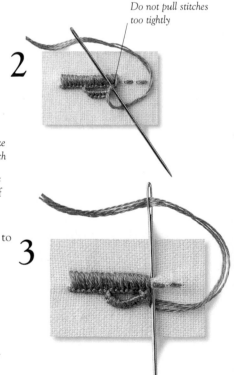

2

3

1 Sew a line of closely spaced running stitch (see p.39) along the edge to be worked. Make a row of buttonhole stitch (see p.58) over it, finishing at the right edge of the picot, at **A**. Take the needle back to **B** and pass it under the horizontal thread to form the foundation loop. Slide the needle under the loop from right to left, over the working thread and gently pull through.

2 Work a series of buttonhole stitches to cover the foundation loop.

3 Continue working buttonhole stitch along the marked line. When complete, carefully trim away the surplus fabric using sharp embroidery scissors.

Buttonhole Eyelet

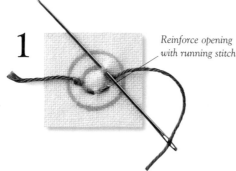

Reinforce opening with running stitch

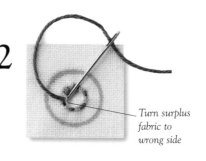

Turn surplus fabric to wrong side

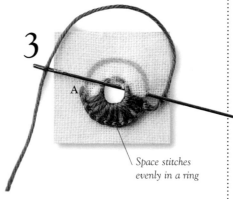

A

Space stitches evenly in a ring

···· LEVEL ····
Advanced

········· USES ·········
Circular holes; laced eyelets

······ METHOD ·······
Buttonhole stitch worked in a ring around central opening

······ MATERIALS ······
Closely woven fabric; any fine thread; sharp scissors

1 Mark two concentric circles on the fabric. Outline the inner circle with a round of closely spaced running stitch (see p.39).

2 Clip the knot and make two cuts at right angles across the inner circle. Using the point of the needle, ease the fabric to the wrong side and finger press in place.

3 Come up at **A** on the outer circle and work a circle of buttonhole stitch (see p.58) into the centre. Trim any surplus fabric on the wrong side.

Overcast Eyelet

A

Do not leave any space between stitches

···· LEVEL ····
Advanced

········· USES ·········
Broderie Anglaise; openwork

······· METHOD ·······
Small open circle with bound edge

······ MATERIALS ······
Fine cotton or linen; any fine thread

Draw a circle onto the fabric and prepare as for steps 1 and 2 above. Bring the needle up a short distance away from the folded edge, at **A** and work a ring of short stitches into the space.

Square Eyelet

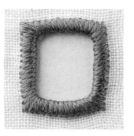

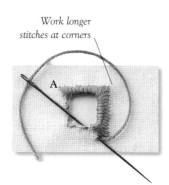

Work longer stitches at corners

A

···· LEVEL ····
Advanced

········· USES ·········
Broderie Anglaise; openwork

······· METHOD ·······
Cut square with bound edge

······ MATERIALS ······
Any fine fabric; fine thread

Mark the outline and work a round of running stitch over it. Make two diagonal cuts across the square and finger press the surplus fabric to the wrong side. Come up at **A** and work a round of straight stitches into the opening, angling them at each corner.

NEEDLEPOINT

STRAIGHT NEEDLEPOINT STITCHES

· · · · · · · · ◆ · · · · · · ·

DIAGONAL NEEDLEPOINT STITCHES

· · · · · · · · ◆ · · · · · · ·

CROSS AND STAR
NEEDLEPOINT STITCHES

· · · · · · · · ◆ · · · · · · ·

LOOPED AND TIED
NEEDLEPOINT STITCHES

Straight Needlepoint Stitches

THIS VERSATILE GROUP of stitches includes stripes, zigzags, diamonds and other geometric patterns which can be used for fillings and backgrounds on various scales, using one or more colours. They are all stitched either horizontally or vertically, so that the thread lies parallel to the grain of the canvas. This means that they do not distort the square weave in the same way as diagonal stitches and, with care, they can be worked without a frame. The stitches are all sewn on single canvas, and the thread, yarn or wool used must be thick enough to conceal the background completely.

Upright Gobelin

····· OTHER NAME ·····
Straight Gobelin stitch

········ LEVEL ·········
Easy

········· USES ·········
Ridged fillings and backgrounds

······· METHOD ·······
Horizontal rows of vertical straight stitches, worked alternately from right to left

······ MATERIALS ······
Single canvas; any thread

Work each stitch over four threads

Starting at top left, make an upright stitch from **5A** to **1A** and repeat to the end of the line. Begin the next row at **9F** to **5F** and stitch towards the left. Repeat these two rows to fill the required area.

Gobelin Filling

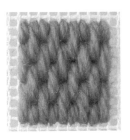

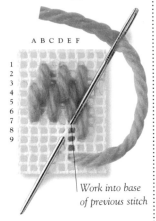

········ LEVEL ·········
Easy

········· USES ·········
Twill effect backgrounds and shaded fillings

······· METHOD ·······
Interlocking horizontal rows of upright stitches

······ MATERIALS ······
Single canvas; any thread

Work into base of previous stitch

Start at top left. Work the first stitch from **7A** to **3A**, the second from **5B** to **1B** and repeat to the end of the line. Begin the next row at **9F** to **5F** and **11E** to **7E** and work towards the left; repeat these two rows to continue.

Parisian

········· LEVEL ·········
Easy

········· USES ·········
Textured fillings and large background areas

······· METHOD ·······
Interlocking horizontal rows of alternate long and short upright stiches

······ MATERIALS ······
Single canvas; any thread

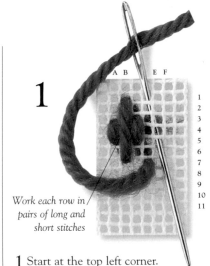

1

Work each row in pairs of long and short stitches

1 Start at the top left corner. Work a short stitch over two threads from **5A** to **3A** and a long stitch over six threads from **7B** to **1B**. Repeat these two stitches to the end of the line.

2 Begin the next row with a short stitch from **9F** to **7F** and a long stitch from **11E** to **5E**, then work alternate long and short stitches to the end of the row. Repeat these two steps to fill the required area.

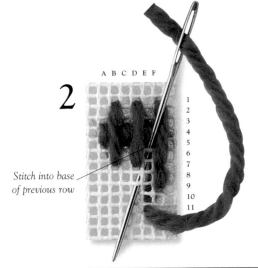

2

Stitch into base of previous row

····· TECHNIQUE VARIATION ·····

To create a secondary pattern within Parisian stitch, work all the long stitches in a dark yarn, then fill the spaces with short stitches in a contrasting colour.

Hungarian

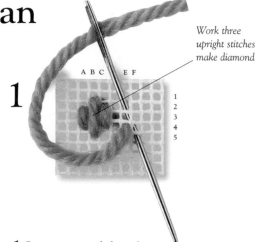

Work three upright stitches to make diamond

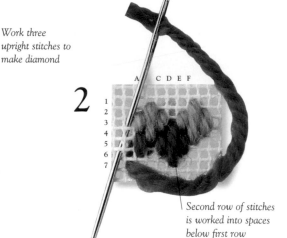

Second row of stitches is worked into spaces below first row

········ Level ········
Easy

········ Uses ········
Textured fillings

······ Method ······
Horizontal rows of small interlocking diamonds

······ Materials ······
Single canvas; any thread in one or two colours

1 Starting at top left, make a short stitch over two threads from **4A** to **2A**. Work a long stitch from **5B** to **1B**, then another short stitch from **4C** to **2C**. Miss one space, then come up at **4E** to start the next diamond. Continue to the end of the line.

2 Using a contrasting colour, come up at **6E** to start the next row. Repeat the sequence of three stitches and one space, working from right to left.

········ TECHNIQUE VARIATION ········

When Hungarian stitch is worked in just a single colour it produces a smooth, brocade-like texture which provides a good background for detailed tent stitch designs.

Hungarian Diamond

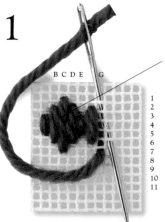

Work progressively longer and shorter stitches

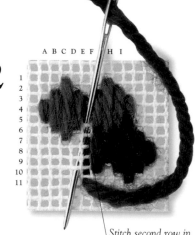

Stitch second row in opposite direction, working into spaces left below first

········ Level ········
Easy

········ Uses ········
Striped backgrounds and fillings

······ Method ······
Hungarian stitch variation on larger scale

······ Materials ······
Single canvas; any thread

1 Start at top left. Work three progressively longer stitches from **5A** to **3A**, **6B** to **2B** and **7C** to **1C**, then a shorter stitch from **6D** to **2D**. Repeat these four stitches to the end of the row and work two shorter stitches to complete the final diamond.

2 Use a second colour for the next row. Start with a short stitch from **9K** to **7K** and continue as above, working from right to left. Repeat these two rows to fill the required area.

Single Twill

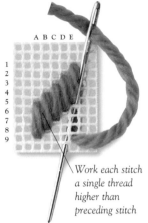

········· LEVEL ·········
Easy

········· USES ·········
Ridged fillings and woven effect backgrounds

········ METHOD ········
Diagonal rows of vertical straight stitches

······· MATERIALS ·······
Single canvas; any thread

Work each stitch a single thread higher than preceding stitch

Start at the top left with a straight stitch from **9A** to **5A**. Work the next from **8B** to **4B** and continue stitching upwards. Start the next row at **9E** to **5E**, and continue working downwards. Repeat these two rows to continue.

Double Twill

········· LEVEL ·········
Easy

········· USES ·········
Textured fillings and backgrounds

········ METHOD ········
Alternate rows of long and short upright stitches, worked diagonally

······· MATERIALS ·······
Single canvas; any thread

Work short stitches over two threads

Work the first row as for single twill stitch (see above). Start the second row with **7E** to **5E** and continue working short stitches downwards. Repeat these two rows to fill the required area.

Bargello

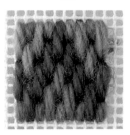

1

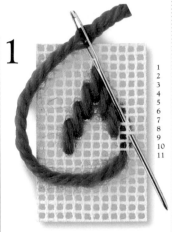

····· OTHER NAMES ·····
Florentine stitch; flame stitch

········· LEVEL ·········
Easy

········· USES ·········
Large patterned areas

········ METHOD ········
Straight stitch worked in wide zigzag bands

······· MATERIALS ·······
Single canvas; any yarn in a selection of toning and contrasting colours

2

Insert needle into base of previous stitch

1 Start at the left with a straight stitch from **11A** to **7A**. Make three stitches upwards from **9B** to **5B**, **7C** to **3C** and **5D** to **1D**. Work the next three stitches downwards, leaving two threads between each, ending at **7G**. Come up at **9H** and repeat this sequence to the end of the row.

2 Stitch the next row in the same way, starting at **15A** and using a lighter shade of the same colour. The third row is worked in a paler yarn, starting at **19A**. Repeat these three rows to continue.

················ TECHNIQUE VARIATION················

To create a wider zigzag with a stepped effect, work blocks of two and three stitches in the centre of the diagonals. Add in a contrasting colour yarn to give more visual interest.

Chevron

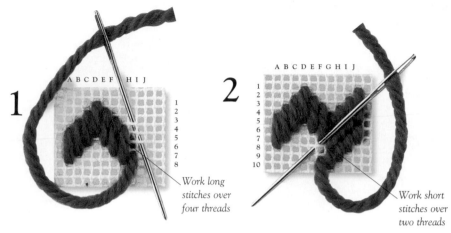

·········· LEVEL ··········
Easy

·········· USES ··········
Backgrounds and fillings

·········· METHOD ··········
*Alternate zigzag bands of
long and short stitches*

·········· MATERIALS ··········
*Single canvas; any thread
in one or two colours*

*Work long
stitches over
four threads*

*Work short
stitches over
two threads*

1 Start at the top left corner with a stitch from
8A to **4A**. Work three more stitches upwards
from **7B** to **3B**, **6C** to **2C** and **5D** to **1D**, then
two downwards stitches from **6E** to **2E** and **7F** to
3F. Repeat this sequence to the end of the row.

2 Begin the next row with a short stitch from **7J**
to **5J**. Continue stitching from right to left,
working into the base of the previous row. Repeat
these two rows to continue.

·········· TECHNIQUE VARIATION ··········

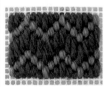

Emphasise the zigzag
pattern within
chevron stitch by
working alternate
rows in different
colour threads.

Hungarian Ground

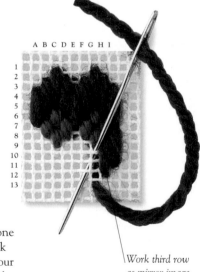

·········· LEVEL ··········
Intermediate

·········· USES ··········
Geometric fillings

·········· METHOD ··········
*Alternate straight stitch
zigzags and diamonds*

·········· MATERIALS ··········
Single canvas; any thread

*Work diamond block of
four short stitches into
space below chevron*

*Work third row
as mirror image
of first*

1 Start at the top left corner. Work three long stitches
upwards from **7A** to **3A**, **6B** to **2B** and **5C** to **1C** and one
stitch downwards from **6D** to **2D**, then repeat this block
to the end of the line. Using the second colour, make four
short stitches from **8H** to **6H**, **7G** to **5G**, **9G** to **7G** and
8F to **6F**. Start the next diamond at **8D**.

2 With the first colour, work three stitches downwards
from **11I** to **7I**, **12H** to **8H** and **13G** to **9G**, then two
stitches upwards from **12F** to **8F** and **11E** to **7E**. Repeat to
the end of the row, then fill in the spaces with diamonds.

Straight Cushion

·········· LEVEL ··········
Intermediate

·········· USES ··········
Chequerboard fillings

········ METHOD ········
*Alternate rows of
diamonds worked in long
and short straight stitches*

········ MATERIALS ········
*Single canvas; any thread
or yarn in two colours*

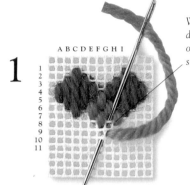

1

A B C D E F G H I

1 2 3 4 5 6 7 8 9 10 11

*Work three
diagonal rows
of three short
stitches*

2

A B C D E F G H I J

1 2 3 4 5 6 7 8 9 10 11 12 13

*Stitch third row of
diamonds directly
below first diamonds*

1 Work the first row as step 1 of Scottish diamond stitch (see below) starting at **5A**. Using a second colour, work three rows of stitches, from **8H** to **6H**, **7G** to **5G**, **6F** to **4F**; **7E** to **5E**, **8F** to **6F**, **9G** to **7G** and **10F** to **8F**, **9E** to **7E** and **8D** to **6D**.

2 Work the third row as the first, starting at **11K** and stitching from right to left. Continue working alternate rows of dark and light diamonds.

·········· TECHNIQUE VARIATION ··········

Work straight cushion stitch in two shades of the same colour, instead of two contrasting yarns, to give a subtle brocade effect for fillings or large-scale backgrounds.

Scottish Diamond

·········· LEVEL ··········
Intermediate

·········· USES ··········
*Textured fillings and
backgrounds*

········ METHOD ········
*Straight stitch chevrons
and diamonds worked in
alternate rows*

········ MATERIALS ········
Single canvas; any thread

1

*Make five stitches
for each diamond*

1 2 3 4 5 6 7 8 9

A B C D E F G H I J K L M

2

A B C D E F G H I J K L M

1 2 3 4 5 6 7 8 9 10 11

*Work short
stitches over
two threads*

1 Start at top left. Work five upright stitches in a diamond shape from **7B** to **5B**, **8C** to **4C**, **9D** to **3D**, **8E** to **4E** and **7F** to **5F**. Repeat to the end of the line, leaving one space between each diamond.

2 Work a zigzag line above and below the diamonds. Start at **4A** to **6A**, then work three stitches upwards from **3B** to **5B**, **2C** to **4C** and **1D** to **3D**, and two downwards from **2E** to **4E** and **3F** to **5F**. Repeat to the end of the row, then work a mirror image below, starting at **8M** to **6M**. Continue working alternate rows of diamonds and chevrons to fill the required area.

Diamond

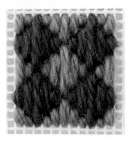

··········· LEVEL ···········
Easy

··········· USES ···········
Fillings and backgrounds

··········· METHOD ···········
*Large-scale variation of
Hungarian stitch*

··········· MATERIALS ···········
*Single canvas; any thread
in one or two colours*

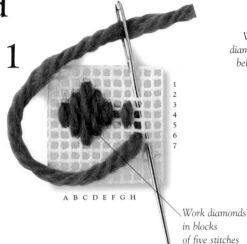

*Work each line of
diamonds into spaces
below previous row*

*Work diamonds
in blocks
of five stitches*

*Stitch second
row in opposite
direction*

1 Start at top left. Work five upright stitches from **5A** to **3A**, **6B** to **2B**, **7C** to **1C**, **6D** to **2D** and **5E** to **3E**. Repeat to the end of the line, leaving one space between each block.

2 The second row is worked from right to left, using the same or a different colour. Start the first block at **8N** to **6N**, then repeat these two rows to continue.

Long Stitch Triangles

··········· LEVEL ···········
Easy

··········· USES ···········
*Textured single-colour
background or filling*

··········· METHOD ···········
*Two rows of interlocking
straight stitch triangles,
repeated horizontally*

··········· MATERIALS ···········
Single canvas; any thread

*Work eight
upright stitches
to form first
triangle*

*Make longest stitches
below shortest stitches of
previous row*

*Stitch second row
from right to left*

1 Start in the top left corner with five progressively longer stitches, worked from **2A** to **1A**, **3B** to **1B**, **4C** to **1C**, **5D** to **1D** and **6E** to **1E**. Work three shorter stitches from **5F** to **1F**, **4G** to **1G** and **3H** to **1H**. Repeat this block to the end of the line.

2 Make a long stitch from **7Q** to **2Q**, then work four shorter stitches from **7P** to **3P**, **7O** to **4O**, **7N** to **5N** and **7M** to **6M**, and three longer stitches from **7L** to **5L**, **7K** to **4K** and **7J** to **3J**. Repeat these two rows to fill the required area.

Lozenge

Work ten vertical stitches to make each diamond

Stitch into base of stitches in previous row

········ LEVEL ········
Intermediate

·········· USES ··········
Harlequin filling or back-ground for large areas

········ METHOD ········
Elongated diamonds, worked in interlocking diagonal rows

······ MATERIALS ·······
Single canvas; two colours of any thread

1 Start at bottom left with five stitches from **11A** to **10A**, **11B** to **9B**, **11C** to **8C**, **11D** to **7D** and **11E** to **6E**. Complete the diamond with five more stitches from **11F** to **6F**, **10G** to **6G**, **9H** to **6H**, **8I** to **6I** and **7J** to **6J**. Begin the next diamond at **6K** to **5K** and contine working upwards.

2 Using a different colour, begin the second row at **11G** to **10G**. Work the third row in the first colour, starting at **11M** to **10M**. Fill in the required space above the stitches with further rows in alternate colours.

Straight Milanese

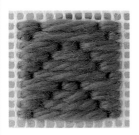

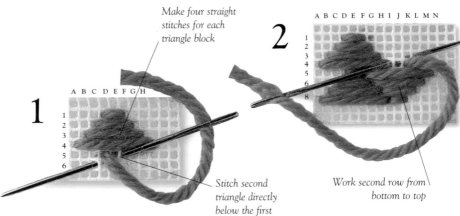

Make four straight stitches for each triangle block

Stitch second triangle directly below the first

Work second row from bottom to top

········ LEVEL ········
Intermediate

·········· USES ··········
Background or filling

········ METHOD ········
Interlocking rows of triangles worked vertically to create a wave pattern

······ MATERIALS ·······
Single canvas; any thread in one or two colours

1 Start at top left. Work four horizontal stitches from **1D** to **1F**, **2C** to **2G**, **3B** to **3H** and **4A** to **4I**. Begin the next triangle at **5D** to **5F** and continue downwards to the end of the row.

2 Begin the next row with four stitches from **8K** to **8I**, **7L** to **7H**, **6M** to **6G** and **5N** to **5F**. Continue working upwards, then repeat these two rows to fill the required area.

········ TECHNIQUE VARIATION ········

For a more geometric effect, work alternate rows in contrasting or toning colours, to emphasize the triangular formation of straight milanese stitch.

Double Brick

···· OTHER NAME ····
Double Gobelin filling

···· LEVEL ····
Easy

···· USES ····
Single colour filling

···· METHOD ····
*Interlocking rows of
double straight stitches*

···· MATERIALS ····
Single canvas; any thread

*Work each
upright stitch
over four threads*

*Stitch second row
from right to left*

1 Start at top left. Work two parallel stitches from **5A** to **1A** and **5B** to **1B**, then two more from **7C** to **3C** and **7D** to **7D**. Come up at **5E** and continue working pairs of staggered straight stitches to the end of the row.

2 Work the second and subsequent rows in the same way, starting with a pair of stitches from **9J** to **5J** and **9I** to **5I**.

Brick Filling

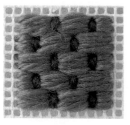

···· LEVEL ····
Intermediate

···· USES ····
Small-scale fillings

···· METHOD ····
*Pairs of horizontal
straight stitches divided by
vertical stitches*

···· MATERIALS ····
*Single canvas; any thread
in two colours*

*Work each
horizontal stitch
over four threads*

*Work each upright
stitch over one thread*

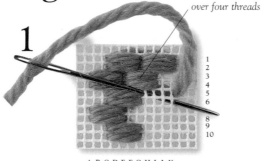

*Avoid catching long
stitches with needle*

1 Starting at bottom left, work two horizontal stitches from **10G** to **10C** and **9G** to **9C**, then a second staggered pair from **8E** to **8A** and **7E** to **7A**. Continue upwards, then work the second row downwards in the same way, starting at **1K** to **1G**. Repeat these two rows to fill the required area.

2 Using a contrasting thread, work short upright stitches at the points where pairs of stitches meet, starting with **1G** to **2G**.

···· TECHNIQUE VARIATION ····

Working the vertical stitches (see step 2, above) in the same thread as the horizontal stitches produces a more textured surface with a quilted appearance.

Long and Short Brick

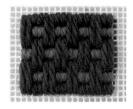

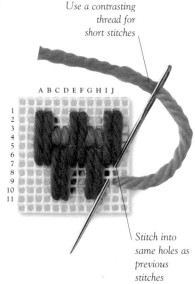

Leave two spaces between each pair of straight stitches

Work each long stitch over six horizontal threads

Use a contrasting thread for short stitches

Stitch into same holes as previous stitches

····· OTHER NAME ·····
Brick stitch

········ LEVEL ········
Intermediate

········· USES ·········
Fillings and backgrounds

······· METHOD ·······
Alternate pairs of long and short stitches

····· MATERIALS ·····
Single canvas; one or two colours of any thread

1 Start at top left and work two stitches from **7A** to **1A** and **7B** to **1B**. Make two more from **7E** to **1E** and **7F** to **1F**. Repeat to the end of the row, leaving two spaces between each pair of stitches. Start the next row with **11H** to **5H** and **11G** to **5G** and continue working from right to left.

2 Fill in the spaces with pairs of short stitches, starting with **5C** to **3C** and **5D** to **3D**. Repeat these two steps to continue.

Basket Filling

Slip needle under vertical stitch before inserting

Work each stitch over six threads

········ LEVEL ·········
Intermediate

·········· USES ··········
Large-scale woven-look filling or background

······· METHOD ·······
Straight stitch worked in alternate vertical and horizontal blocks

······ MATERIALS ······
Single canvas; any thread

1 Start at top left. Work a block of five upright stitches from **7B** to **1B**, **7C** to **1C**, **7D** to **1D**, **7E** to **1E** and **7F** to **1F**, then work a block of five horizontal stitches from **2L** to **2F**, **3L** to **3F**, **4L** to **4F**, **5L** to **5F** and **6L** to **6F**. Repeat to the end of the line.

2 Work five upright stitches below the horizontal block, starting with **12K** to **6K** and ending with **12G** to **6G**. Work a horizontal block under the upright block, starting at **7A** to **7F** and ending with **12A** to **12F**. Repeat to the end of the line, then repeat these two rows to continue.

Diagonal Needlepoint Stitches

THIS SECTION STARTS with tent stitch and its variations, which are the most frequently used needlepoint stitches. Like all the other diagonal stitches, they are worked at a slant across the thread intersections. This can have the effect of distorting the square weave of the canvas, even when it is mounted in a frame. The finished piece should be stretched and blocked back into shape. Some diagonal stitches are worked on single canvas, others on double. Always match the thickness of the thread or yarn to the weight of the canvas being used, so that no background threads are visible.

Half Cross

····· LEVEL ·····
Easy

········· USES ·········
Charts; printed canvases

····· METHOD ·····
Small slanting stitches

····· MATERIALS ·····
Double canvas; thick yarn

········· TIP ·········
Turn work upside-down for return journey to stitch rows in same direction

Start at top left. Stitch over one intersection, from **2A** to **1B** and **2B** to **1C**, then repeat to the end of the line. Begin the next row with **2F** to **3E** and **2E** to **3D**. Repeat these two rows to continue.

Basketweave Tent

···· OTHER NAMES ····
Continental stitch; diagonal tent stitch

········· LEVEL ·········
Intermediate

········· USES ·········
Backgrounds and fillings

········· METHOD ·········
Tent stitch worked in diagonal rows

········· MATERIALS ·······
Single canvas; any thread

Starting at top right, make a stitch from **2E** to **1F**. Work the next row upwards from **3E** to **2F** and **2D** to **1E** and the third downwards from **2C** to **1D**, **3D** to **2E** and **4E** to **3F**. Begin the following row with **5E** to **4F**: continue working up, then down.

Tent

····· OTHER NAME ·····
Petit point

········· LEVEL ·········
Easy

········· USES ·········
Backgrounds; detailed charted or printed patterns

········· METHOD ·········
Worked horizontally

····· MATERIALS ·····
Single canvas; any thread

Take needle behind two threads to make long stitch on reverse side

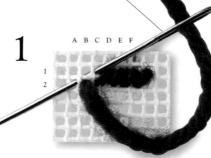

1 Start at top right and sew a diagonal stitch from **2F** to **1G**. Work the second stitch from **2E** to **1F** and repeat to the end of the row.

2 Turn the canvas the other way up and repeat step 1 or work the second row from left to right, starting with **2B** to **3A**. Repeat these two rows.

Work each stitch in same direction

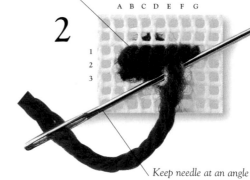

Keep needle at an angle

···············STITCH VARIATION···············

Trammed tent stitch is sewn over long straight stitches worked through the small holes on a double canvas. This gives a ridged effect and because it is hardwearing, this stitch is often used for seat covers.

Gobelin

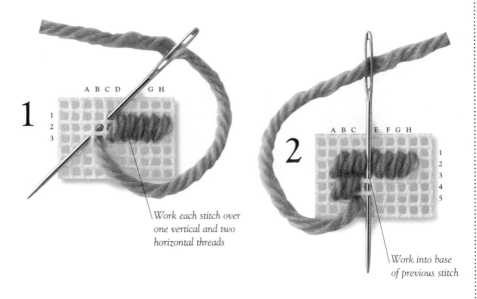

····· OTHER NAMES ·····
Oblique Gobelin;
gros point

····· LEVEL ·····
Easy

······ USES ·····
Backgrounds and fillings

······ METHOD ·····
Long diagonal stitches
worked in horizontal rows

······ MATERIALS ·····
Single canvas, any thread

Work each stitch over
one vertical and two
horizontal threads

Work into base
of previous stitch

1 Start at top right. Make the first diagonal stitch from **3G** to **1H** and the next from **3F** to **1G**. Repeat to the end of the line.

2 Begin the return journey with two stitches from **5A** to **3B** and **5B** to **3C**, and continue to the end of the row. Repeat these two rows to fill the required area.

Encroaching Gobelin

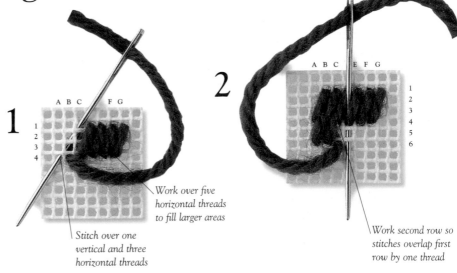

········ LEVEL ·····
Easy

······ USES ·····
Backgrounds; filling for
plain or shaded areas

······ METHOD ·····
Overlapping rows of
diagonal stitches, worked
horizontally

······ MATERIALS ·····
Single canvas; any yarn

Work over five
horizontal threads
to fill larger areas

Stitch over one
vertical and three
horizontal threads

Work second row so
stitches overlap first
row by one thread

1 Starting at top right, work a row of diagonal stitches, beginning with **4F** to **1G** and **4E** to **1F**.

2 Work the first stitch of the next row from **6A** to **3B** and the second from **6B** to **3C**. Continue to the end of the line and repeat these two steps to continue.

Reversed Sloping Gobelin

········· LEVEL ·········
Easy

········· USES ·········
Plain or shaded fillings and backgrounds

········· METHOD ·········
Vertical rows of diagonal straight stitches worked alternately down and up

········· MATERIALS ·········
Any canvas; any thread

1

Make stitch over two thread intersections

2

Work second row at right angles to first

1 Start at top left and work a diagonal stitch from **3C** to **1A**. Work the next stitch from **4C** to **2A** and repeat downwards to the end of the line.

2 Begin the next line with a stitch in the opposite direction from **6E** to **8C**, then continue working upwards. Repeat these two rows.

········· TECHNIQUE VARIATION ·········

To produce a shaded effect, work the stitches in the lower part of the stitched area with a selection of progressively darker tones of the main colour.

Canvas Stem

········· LEVEL ·········
Intermediate

········· USES ·········
Textured background, filling or chevron border

········· METHOD ·········
Two upright rows of diagonal stitches, set in a V-shape, and divided by lines of back stitch

········· MATERIALS ·········
Double canvas; two colours of any yarn

1

Work each stitch over three thread intersections

2

Ensure back stitches conceal horizontal threads

Use contrasting thread for back stitch

1 Starting at top left, make a diagonal stitch from **4D** to **1A**. Work the second stitch directly below, from **5D** to **2A**, and continue stitching downwards. Begin the next row at **6G** to **9D**. Make another stitch from **5G** to **8D** and continue working upwards. Repeat these two rows to cover the required area.

2 Make two back stitches from **4D** to **3D** and **5D** to **4D** and continue downwards. Work further rows of back stitch into the holes between the lines of diagonal stitches.

Florence

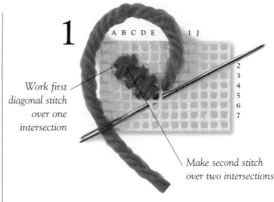

··· OTHER NAME ···
Diagonal mosaic stitch

········ LEVEL ········
Easy

········· USES ·········
Plain or striped fillings

······· METHOD ·······
Alternate long and short slanting stitches, worked diagonally

····· MATERIALS ······
Any canvas; any thread

Work first diagonal stitch over one intersection

Make second stitch over two intersections

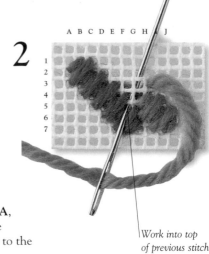

Work into top of previous stitch

1 Start at top left. Make a short stitch from **1B** to **2A**, followed by a longer stitch from **1C** to **3A**. Continue working alternate long and short stitches downwards to the bottom edge of the area being filled.

2 The next row is worked upwards using the same or a different colour yarn. Begin with a short stitch from **6J** to **7I** and a long one from **5J** to **7H** and repeat to the end of the row. Repeat these two steps to continue.

Cashmere

········ LEVEL ········
Easy

········· USES ·········
Textured plain or striped backgrounds and fillings

······· METHOD ·······
Groups of three diagonal stitches worked vertically

····· MATERIALS ······
Any canvas; any thread

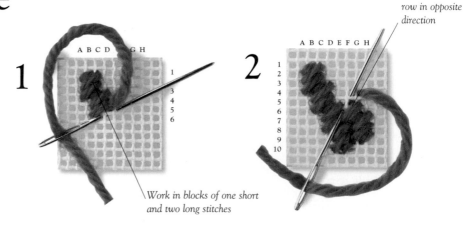

Work in blocks of one short and two long stitches

Stitch second row in opposite direction

1 Starting at top left, make a short diagonal stitch from **1B** to **2A**. Work two longer stitches from **1C** to **3A** and **2C** to **4A**. Repeat these three stitches, working downwards to the end of the row.

2 The next row is worked upwards. Make a short stitch from **8H** to **9G** and the next two long stitches from **7H** to **9F** and **6H** to **8F**. Repeat steps 1 and 2 to fill the required area.

····· TECHNIQUE VARIATION ·····

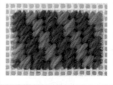

Work alternate rows in a second colour to create a pattern of ridged diagonal stripes.

Diagonal

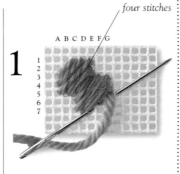

Work in blocks of four stitches

1

A B C D E F G

2

A B C D E F G H I J K

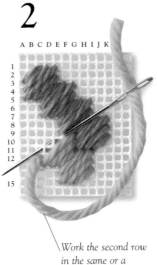

Work the second row in the same or a contrasting colour

········ LEVEL ········
Easy

········ USES ········
Plain or striped filling or background for large areas

········ METHOD ········
Graduated straight stitches worked in diagonal rows

········ MATERIALS ········
Any canvas; one or two colours of any thread

1 Start at the top left corner. Each row is made up of blocks of four stitches, beginning with **1C** to **3A**, **1D** to **4A**, **1E** to **5A** and **2E** to **5B**. Work the first stitch of the next block from **3E** to **5C** and continue working downwards.

2 The next row is worked upwards in the same way. Make the first block from **13I** to **15G**, **12I** to **15F**, **11I** to **15E** and **11H** to **14E**. Repeat these two rows to continue and fill in the spaces with additional diagonal stitches (see p.19).

····················· TECHNIQUE VARIATION ·····················

For a more unusual effect, use one colour to sew the diagonal stitch, then work rows of contrasting back stitch (see p.40) between the lines. This will conceal any canvas that may show through and creates the illusion of a set of diagonal laid threads couched by zigzag lines of back stitch.

Byzantine

1

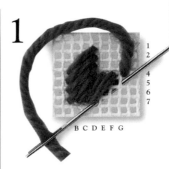

B C D E F G

2

A B C D E F G H I J K L M

···· OTHER NAME ····
Step stitch

········ LEVEL ········
Easy

········ USES ········
Large scale fillings and backgrounds

········ METHOD ········
Diagonal straight stitches, worked in zigzag lines

········ MATERIALS ········
Any canvas; any thread

3

A B C D E F G H I J K L M N O P

1 Start at top left. Each zigzag is made up of repeated blocks of six diagonal stitches. Work the first four stitches downwards from **1D** to **4A**, **2D** to **5A**, **3D** to **6A** and **4D** to **7A**. The next two stitches are worked to the right, from **4E** to **7B** and **4F** to **7C**. Start the next block at **4G**.

2 Work the second row level with and to the right of the first, starting at **1J** to **4G**. Make further rows to the right to fill the area required.

3 Complete any space at the bottom left corner with extra zigzags, starting at **10A** to **7D**, then work short stitches to fill the gaps (see p.19).

Jacquard

········· LEVEL ·········
Intermediate

········· USES ·········
*Zigzag filling for
large areas*

········· METHOD ·········
*Stepped rows of alternate
diagonal and tent stitch*

········· MATERIALS ·········
*Single canvas; one or two
colours of any thread*

1

*Make eight
stitches for
each block*

2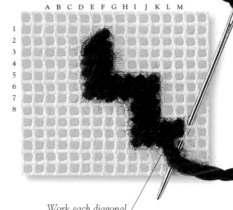

*Work each diagonal
stitch over two
intersections*

3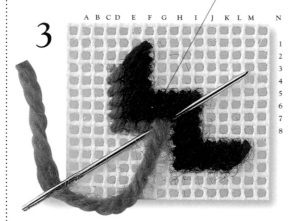

*Work tent stitch
over one intersection*

4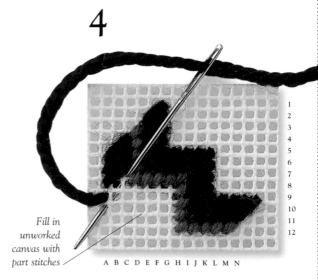

*Fill in
unworked
canvas with
part stitches*

········· TECHNIQUE VARIATION ·········

Work this stitch in one
single colour to create a
brocade-like background.
Lustrous threads give a
smooth, shiny surface
that will add to the woven effect.

1 Start at top left. Work a block of five diagonal stitches downwards from **3D** to **1F**, **4D** to **2F**, **5D** to **3F**, **6D** to **4F** and **7D** to **5F**, and three to the right from **7E** to **5G**, **7F** to **5H** and **7G** to **5I**.

2 Repeat this block to the bottom right corner of the area to be filled.

3 Using the second colour, work a block of five tent stitches downwards from **4C** to **3D**, **5C** to **4D**, and **6C** to **5D**, **7C** to **6D** and **8C** to **7D** and three to the right from **8D** to **7E**, **8E** to **7F**, **8F** to **7G**. Repeat this block to the end of the row.

4 Repeat step 1, starting with **6A** to **4C**, then continue working these two rows in alternate colours to fill the space.

Moorish

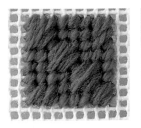

········ LEVEL ········
Intermediate

········ USES ········
*Large-scale filling with
zigzag pattern*

········ METHOD ········
*Alternate rows of
graduated diagonal
stitches and tent stitch*

········ MATERIALS ········
*Any canvas; any thread
in one or two colours*

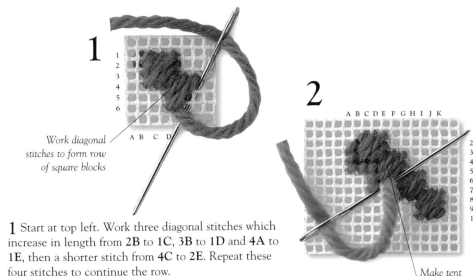

1

*Work diagonal
stitches to form row
of square blocks*

A B C D

2

A B C D E F G H I J K

*Make tent
stitch over one
intersection*

1 Start at top left. Work three diagonal stitches which increase in length from **2B** to **1C**, **3B** to **1D** and **4A** to **1E**, then a shorter stitch from **4C** to **2E**. Repeat these four stitches to continue the row.

2 Using the second thread, work a stepped line of tent stitch to the left of the first row. Start with **2B** to **3A**, **3B** to **4A**, **4B** to **5A** and **4C** to **5B**, then repeat these four stitches. Repeat steps 1 and 2 to continue, working each successive row into the spaces left by the row before.

Milanese

········ LEVEL ········
Intermediate

········ USES ········
*Brocade-like background
or filling for larger areas*

········ METHOD ········
*Diagonal rows of
alternate long and short
back stitch forming
triangular pattern*

········ MATERIALS ········
Any canvas; any thread

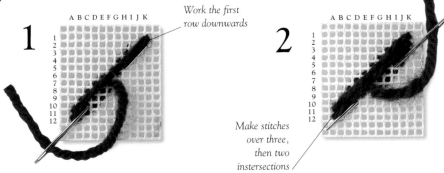

1

A B C D E F G H I J K

*Work the first
row downwards*

2

A B C D E F G H I J K

*Make stitches
over three,
then two
intersections*

3

A B C D E F G H I J K

1 Start at top right. Work a long stitch from **5G** to **1K** and a short stitch from **6F** to **5G**, then repeat these two stitches to the end of the line. Start the next row with a short stitch from **10C** to **12A** and a long stitch from **7F** to **10C**, and repeat these two stitches, working upwards.

2 Start the third row with **5I** to **3K** and **8F** to **5I**, and repeat these two stitches, working downwards.

3 Work the fourth row upwards, starting with **10E** to **14A** and **9F** to **10E**. Repeat these four rows to continue.

Mosaic

.... Level ....
Easy

.... Uses ....
Fine textured backgrounds

.... Method ....
Long and short diagonal
stitches worked in
horizontal rows to form
square pattern

.... Materials ....
Any canvas, any thread

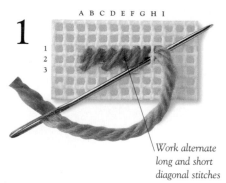

A B C D E F G H I

1
2
3

1

*Work alternate
long and short
diagonal stitches*

*Fill in spaces
with short
stitches*

A B C D E F G H I

1
2
3

2

1 Start at top left with two diagonal stitches from **1B** to **2A** and **1C** to **3A**. Repeat these two stitches to the end of the line.

2 Work the second row in the opposite direction. Make a short stitch from **3H** to **2I** to complete the first square, then continue working towards the left. Repeat these two rows to fill the required area.

········· Technique Variation·········

Change the visual effect by working the squares in two or more toning or contrasting colours to make a chequerboard pattern, ideal for filling smaller areas.

Cushion

.... Level ....
Easy

.... Uses ....
Filling or background with
regular pattern of squares

.... Method ....
Graduated diagonal
stitches worked in squares

.... Materials ....
Any canvas; any thread

A B C D E

1
2
3
4

1

*Work diagonal
stitches to form
a square block*

A B C D E F G H I J

1
2
3
4
5

2

1 Starting at the top left corner, work five stitches from **1B** to **2A**, **1C** to **3A**, **1D** to **4A**, **2D** to **4B** and **3D** to **4C**. Start the next block at **1E** to **2D** and continue to the end of the row.

2 Work the second row in the opposite direction, starting at **5G** to **4H**. Repeat steps 1 and 2 until the required space is filled.

········· Technique Variation·········

To prevent the canvas distorting, the square blocks can be worked in alternate directions using one or two colours.

Scottish

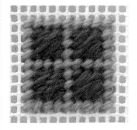

·········· LEVEL ··········
Intermediate

·········· USES ··········
Filling for large areas

········ METHOD ········
*Cushion stitches framed
with a line of tent stitch*

········ MATERIALS ········
Any canvas; any thread

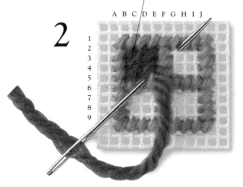

*Make five diagonal
stitches to fill square*

*Work tent stitch
over one thread
intersection*

1 Starting at top left, work the tent stitch frame
(see p.129). Make a grid of horizontal and vertical
rows, leaving a square of three canvas threads
between the lines.

2 Fill the squares with cushion stitch (see p.136),
using a second colour. Work the first block from **2C**
to **3B**, **2D** to **4B**, **2E** to **5B**, **3E** to **5C** and **4E** to
5D, then come up at **2G** to start the next square.

Chequer

·········· LEVEL ··········
Intermediate

·········· USES ··········
Textured fillings

········ METHOD ········
*Alternate large
cushion stitches and
square tent stitch blocks*

········ MATERIALS ········
*Any canvas; any thread
in one or two colours*

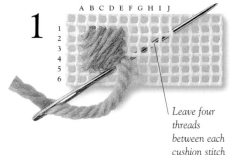

*Leave four
threads
between each
cushion stitch*

*Fill in spaces with
squares of tent stitch*

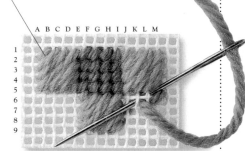

1 Start at top left with the first cushion stitch. Make seven
diagonal stitches from **1B** to **2A**, **1C** to **3A**, **1D** to **4A**, **1E** to
5A, **2E** to **5B**, **3E** to **5C** and **4E** to **5D**. Begin the next block
with **1J** to **2I** and start the next row at **6E** to **5F**.

2 Using a second colour, work squares of tent stitch (see
p.139) in the spaces between the cushion stitches. Starting with
2H to **1I**, work four stitches, then work another three rows
directly below. Repeat to fill all the unworked squares.

Cross and Star Needlepoint Stitches

THIS SECTION INCLUDES all the stitches that are worked with a combination of horizontal, vertical and diagonal stitches. The various cross stitches feature two or more straight stitches that cross over each other, while the individual stitches that make up the star stitches radiate from a central point. The heavier cross variations are all worked on double canvas to give better coverage; the other stitches use single canvas. Whichever background is being used, the chosen thread should be thick enough to cover the canvas completely. This group of stitches should all be worked in a frame.

Cross

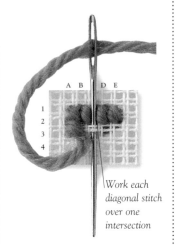

····· OTHER NAME ·····
Berlin stitch

········· LEVEL ··········
Easy

·········· USES ···········
*Charted and printed
designs; backgrounds*

······· METHOD ·······
*Individual cross stitches,
worked horizontally*

······· MATERIALS ·······
*Double canvas; any
thread or yarn*

*Work each
diagonal stitch
over one
intersection*

Start at top right with two
stitches from **1E** to **2D** and
1D to **2E**. Begin the next
cross at **1D** to **2C** and
continue to the left. Work the
first cross of the next row at
3A to **2B** and **3B** to **2A**, then
continue to the right. Repeat
these two rows.

Diagonal Cross

········· LEVEL ··········
Easy

·········· USES ···········
Backgrounds and fillings

······· METHOD ·······
*Single cross stitches,
worked in diagonal rows*

······· MATERIALS ·······
Single canvas; any thread

*Stitch over two
intersections*

Start at bottom left. Work
three crosses from **5A** to **7C**
and **5C** to **7A**; **7E** to **5C** and
7C to **5E**; **5C** to **3A** and **5A**
to **3C**. Begin the next row at
1A to **3C** and **1C** to **3A**, and
start the second cross at **3C**
to **5E**. Repeat these two rows.

Double Cross

········· LEVEL ··········
Intermediate

·········· USES ···········
Two-coloured backgrounds

······· METHOD ·······
*Spaced cross stitches
with overlapping rows of
elongated crosses*

······· MATERIALS ·······
*Double canvas; thin and
thick thread in two colours*

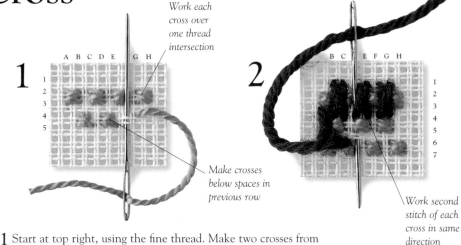

*Work each
cross over
one thread
intersection*

*Make crosses
below spaces in
previous row*

*Work second
stitch of each
cross in same
direction*

1 Start at top right, using the fine thread. Make two crosses from
2H to **3G** and **2G** to **3H**, then **2F** to **3E** and **2E** to **3F** and
continue towards the left. Begin the next row with **4C** to **5B** and
4B to **5C** and **4E** to **5D** and **4D** to **5E**. Repeat these two rows.

2 Fill in the spaces with rows of long crosses in the thick thread,
worked in alternate directions. Start with **4F** to **1G** and **4G** to **1F**
and work towards the left. Begin the next row with a cross from **6A**
to **3B** and **6B** to **3A** and continue towards the right.

Upright Cross

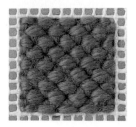

····· OTHER NAME ·····
Straight cross

········· LEVEL ·········
Easy

········· USES ·········
Fine textured backgrounds

······ METHOD ······
Crosses worked singly in interlocking diagonal rows

····· MATERIALS ·····
Any canvas; any thread

Start at top left with two crosses from **3B** to **1B** and **2A** to **2C**, and **4C** to **2C** and **3B** to **3D**; continue downwards. Start the next row with **7D** to **5D** and **6C** to **6E**, **6C** to **4C** and **5B** to **5D** and continue upwards. Repeat these two rows to fill the required area.

Diamond Cross

········· LEVEL ·········
Intermediate

·········· USES ··········
Raised backgrounds and textured fillings

······ METHOD ······
Cross stitches worked over larger upright cross stitches

····· MATERIALS ·····
Single canvas; any thread

Ensure diagonal stitches lie in same direction

Start at top left. Work an upright cross from **3E** to **3A** and **5C** to **1C** covered by a cross from **4D** to **2B** and **4B** to **2D**. Begin the next stitch at **5G** to **5C**, then continue working in diagonal rows.

Smyrna Cross

····· OTHER NAME ·····
Leviathan stitch

········· LEVEL ·········
Easy

·········· USES ··········
Raised backgrounds

········ METHOD ········
Upright cross worked over cross stitch

····· MATERIALS ·····
Single canvas; any thread

1

Work stitch over five thread intersections

1 Start at top left with a diagonal stitch from **1A** to **5E** crossed by a second stitch from **5A** to **1E**. Bring the needle out at **5C**.

2 Make an upright stitch to **1C** and a horizontal stitch from **3A** to **3E**. Bring the needle out at **1E** to begin the next stitch, then continue working in horizontal rows.

Always work stitches in same order

2

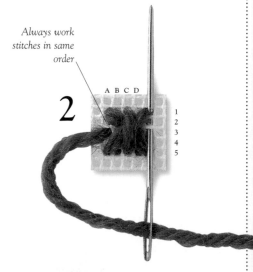

········ TECHNIQUE VARIATION ········

Work alternate crosses in toning or contrasting colours to create an all-over chequer pattern, for a colourful background.

Double Leviathan

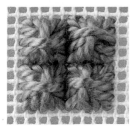

········ LEVEL ········
Intermediate

·········· USES ··········
Highly textured filling

········ METHOD ········
Smyrna cross variation

······ MATERIALS ·······
Single canvas; any yarn or thread – lustrous pearl cotton gives good result

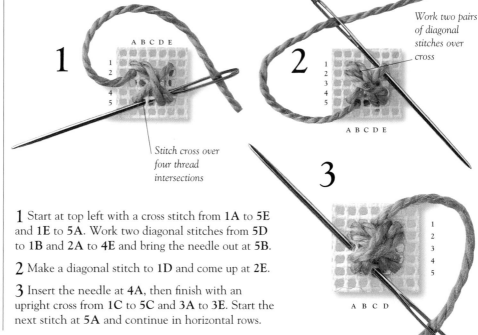

Stitch cross over four thread intersections

Work two pairs of diagonal stitches over cross

1 Start at top left with a cross stitch from **1A** to **5E** and **1E** to **5A**. Work two diagonal stitches from **5D** to **1B** and **2A** to **4E** and bring the needle out at **5B**.

2 Make a diagonal stitch to **1D** and come up at **2E**.

3 Insert the needle at **4A**, then finish with an upright cross from **1C** to **5C** and **3A** to **3E**. Start the next stitch at **5A** and continue in horizontal rows.

Diagonal Tweed

········ LEVEL ········
Intermediate

·········· USES ··········
Two-colour filling with raised surface

········ METHOD ········
Smyrna crosses alternated with large crosses covered by small upright crosses

······ MATERIALS ·······
Single canvas; two colours of any thread

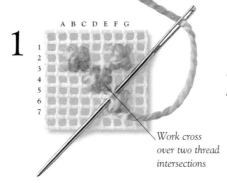

Work cross over two thread intersections

Use a contrasting colour for large double crosses

1 Starting at top left, work a series of small Smyrna cross stitches (see left). Leave two threads between each stitch and work the crosses in subsequent rows beneath these gaps.

2 Using the second thread, work a cross stitch from **6H** to **2D** and **6D** to **2H**. Make a horizontal stitch from **4E** to **4G**, then an upright stitch from **6F** to **3F**. Start the next large cross at **6D** and repeat along the row.

Broad Cross

Work straight stitches over six thread intersections

Insert needle into base of previous row

········· LEVEL ·········
Intermediate

········· USES ···········
Basketweave filling for large areas

········ METHOD ·········
Large square crosses worked in horizontal rows

········· MATERIALS ·······
Single canvas; any thread

1 Start at top left. Work a block of three upright stitches from **7C** to **1C**, **7D** to **1D** and **7E** to **1E**, crossed by three horizontal stitches from **5A** to **5G**, **4A** to **4G** and **3A** to **3G**. Begin the next block at **7I** to **1I** and continue to the end of the row.

2 The second row fits into the spaces between the crosses; begin the first block at **11F** and work subsequent rows in the same way, alternately from right to left.

Cross-corner Cushion

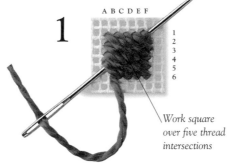

Work square over five thread intersections

Work second layer of stitches at right angles to first

········· LEVEL ·········
Intermediate

·········· USES ············
Filling for large areas

········ METHOD ·········
Cushion stitch variation with two layers of stitches, forming a diagonal pattern

······· MATERIALS ·······
Single canvas; any thread – twisted embroidery cotton gives good results

1 Start at top left with a square of nine graduated diagonal stitches starting at **2F** to **1E** and ending with **6B** to **5A**.

2 Work five more stitches in the opposite direction, from **1F** to **6A**, **2F** to **6B**, **3F** to **6C**, **4F** to **6D** and **5F** to **6E**.

3 Repeat steps 1 and 2 along the row, reversing every other square. Work the next and subsequent rows as a mirror image of the one above.

Brighton

.... LEVEL ....
Intermediate

.... USES ....
*Dense fillings and
backgrounds*

.... METHOD ....
*Straight stitch hexagons,
interspersed with
contrasting upright crosses*

.... MATERIALS ....
*Single canvas; two
colours of any thread*

*Alternate direction
of diagonal stitches
for each block*

*Work upright
cross in space
between diagonal
stitches*

1 Starting at top left, make a hexagonal block of five diagonal stitches from **1C** to **3A**, **1D** to **4A**, **1E** to **5A**, **2E** to **5B** and **3E** to **5C**.

2 Reverse the direction for the second hexagon, starting at **3I** to **1G**. Repeat these two blocks to the end of the line. Work each subsequent row as a mirror image of the one above.

3 Using a contrasting thread, work an upright cross from **4E** to **6E** and **5D** to **5F**. Repeat to fill each space.

Rice

..... OTHER NAME .....
William and Mary stitch

.... LEVEL ....
Intermediate

.... USES ....
Solid lattice filling

.... METHOD ....
*Back stitch square worked
over large cross stitch*

.... MATERIALS ....
*Single canvas; one thick
and one fine thread*

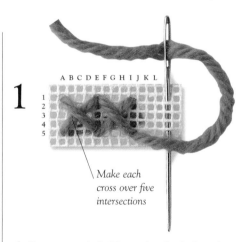

*Make each
cross over five
intersections*

*Work back stitch
in contrasting
colour*

1 Start at top left. Using the thick thread, make a large cross stitch from **5A** to **1E** and **5E** to **1A**. Begin the next cross at **5E** to **1I** and continue along the row.

2 With the fine thread, work four back stitches over the first cross from **3E** to **5C**, **1C** to **3E**, **3A** to **1C** and **5C** to **3A**. Repeat for each cross, starting the next back stitch square at **3I** to **5G**. Work the following rows in the same way, directly below the first.

Plaited Gobelin

········· LEVEL ·········
Easy

········· USES ·········
*Woven effect backgrounds;
filling for large areas*

········· METHOD ·········
*Gobelin variation, worked
in overlapping rows*

········· MATERIALS ·········
*Double canvas; tapestry
yarn or other thick thread*

*Insert needle into
space between
stitches*

*Work in
overlapping
rows to
produce
plaited effect*

1 Start at the top right corner with a diagonal stitch from **3E** to **1D**. Work the next from **3D** to **1C** and continue stitching towards the left.

2 Begin the next row at **4A** to **2B** and repeat this stitch to the end of the row.

3 Work the third row as the first, starting at **5E** to **3D**. Continue working alternately to the left, then right.

Greek

········· LEVEL ·········
Easy

········· USES ·········
*In single rows as outline;
textured filling*

········· METHOD ·········
*Herringbone variation,
worked in horizontal rows*

········· MATERIALS ·········
*Double canvas; any
thick thread*

*Work alternate
long and short
diagonal stitches*

1 Start at top left. Make a short stitch from **1C** to **3A**, then a long stitch from **1A** to **3E**. Come up at **3C**.

2 Make a short stitch to **1E**, then continue working alternate long and short stitches to the end of the line.

3 Work the second row in the opposite direction starting with **5G** to **3E** and **3G** to **5C**. Repeat these two rows to continue.

Plait

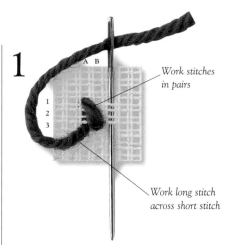

Work stitches in pairs

Work long stitch across short stitch

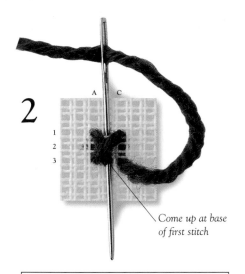

Come up at base of first stitch

········· LEVEL ·········
Easy

·········· USES ··········
Solid ridged backgrounds, in single row as outline

········ METHOD ········
Rows of overlapping straight stitches

······· MATERIALS ·······
Double canvas; any thick thread

1 Start at top left with a diagonal stitch from **3B** to **1A**, crossed by a longer stitch from **3A** to **1C**. Come out at **3C** to start the next pair of stitches.

2 Work a short stitch up to **1B** and come out at **3B**. Continue working pairs of stitches to the end of the line, then stitch the second and subsequent rows directly below the first.

·······TECHNIQUE VARIATION·········

Plait stitch can also be worked in vertical rows, depending on the effect required and the shape of the area to be filled.

Fishbone

Work first row upwards

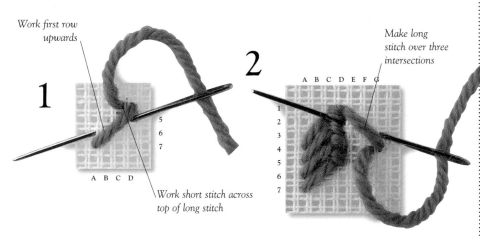

Make long stitch over three intersections

Work short stitch across top of long stitch

········· LEVEL ·········
Intermediate

·········· USES ··········
Textured chevron filling for large areas

········ METHOD ········
Diagonal stitches worked in alternate directions in vertical rows

······· MATERIALS ·······
Double canvas; tapestry yarn or other thick thread

1 Start at bottom left. Make a long diagonal stitch from **7A** to **4D** and a short stitch from **4C** to **5D**. Come up at **6A** and repeat these two stitches to the end of the row.

2 Work the second row downwards. Make the first two stitches from **1D** to **4G** and **4F** to **3G**, then come up at **2D**. Repeat steps 1 and 2 to fill the required area.

·······TECHNIQUE VARIATION·········

Repeat step 1 only to vary the surface of the stitch and work the rows in alternate light and dark colours to make a pattern of bold ridged vertical stripes.

Fern

·········· LEVEL ··········
Easy

·········· USES ··········
*Ridged fillings and
backgrounds*

········· METHOD ·········
*Pairs of overlapping
diagonal stitches worked
in vertical rows*

········ MATERIALS ········
*Double canvas; any thick
thread or yarn*

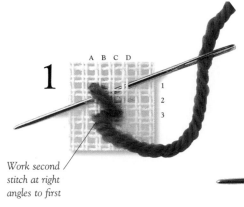

*Work second
stitch at right
angles to first*

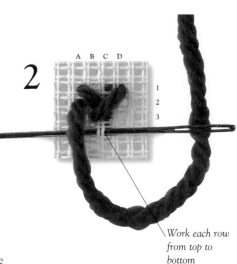

*Work each row
from top to
bottom*

1 Start at top left. Make two diagonal stitches from **1A** to **3C** and **3B** to **1D**. Bring the needle out at **2A** ready to start the next stitches.

2 Work the next pair of stitches directly below the first, from **2A** to **4C** and **4B** to **2D**. Continue working downwards to the end of the row. Start the next row at **1D**.

Fir

········ OTHER NAME ········
Leaf stitch

·········· LEVEL ··········
Intermediate

·········· USES ··········
Filling for large areas

········· METHOD ·········
*Interlocking rows of
hexagonal blocks*

········ MATERIALS ········
Any canvas; any thread

*Work second
side as mirror
image of first*

*Make eleven straight
stitches for each block*

1 Start at top left with an upright stitch from **1D** to **5D**. Work three slanting stitches from **2C** to **5D**, **3B** to **6D** and **4A** to **7D**. Make two more stitches directly below, from **5A** to **8D** and **7A** to **9D**. Come up at **2E**.

2 Make six stitches to mirror step 1 from **2E** to **5D**, to **7G** to **9D**. Start the second block with **1J** to **5J** and continue working to the right. Stitch the next row into the spaces below the first.

······· TECHNIQUE VARIATION ·······

Work an upright stitch from 5D to 9D to vary the leaf shape and stitch the rows in two contrasting colours to create a striped filling.

Rhodes

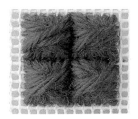

········ LEVEL ········
Intermediate

·········· USES ··········
3-dimensional fillings or background

········ METHOD ········
Raised square stitch worked in straight rows

······ MATERIALS ······
Single canvas; any thread

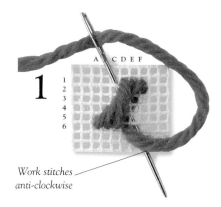

Work stitches anti-clockwise

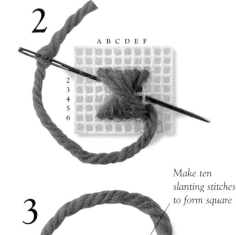

Make ten slanting stitches to form square

Ensure each block is worked in same order

1 Start at top left and work four diagonal stitches from **6A** to **1F**, **6B** to **1E**, **6C** to **1D** and **6D** to **1C**. Come up at **6E**.

2 Work another two stitches from **6E** to **1B**, and **6F** to **1A**. Insert the needle at **1B**, then come up at **4F.**

3 Make three more stitches to complete the square from **4F** to **3A**, **3F** to **4A** and **2F** to **5A**. Come up at **6F**, ready to make the next block. Work the following rows directly below.

Half Rhodes

········ LEVEL ········
Intermediate

·········· USES ··········
Striped raised filling for large areas or backgrounds

········ METHOD ········
Rhodes stitch variation worked in diagonal rows

······ MATERIALS ······
Single canvas; any thread in one or two colours

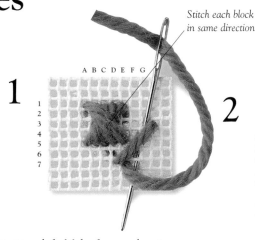

Stitch each block in same direction

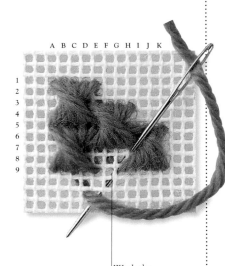

Work the second row into the spaces below the first

1 Start at top left. Make five overlapping straight stitches from **5A** to **1E**, **5B** to **1D**, **5C** to **1C**, **5D** to **1B** and **5E** to **1A**. Come up at **7D** to make the next block, then continue working downwards to the right.

2 Stitch the second row in a different colour, starting at **9A** to **5E**. Work the next and subsequent rows directly below the first.

Star

···· OTHER NAME ····
Algerian eye stitch

···· LEVEL ····
Intermediate

···· USES ····
Fine textured filling

···· METHOD ····
*Straight stitch stars worked
in horizontal rows*

···· MATERIALS ····
Single canvas; thick thread

*Always insert needle
into same hole*

*Work second
star to right
of first*

1 Start at top left with four straight stitches from **1E** to **3C**, **1C** to **3C**, **1A** to **3C** and **3A** to **3C**.

2 Work four more stitches to complete the star, from **5A** to **3C**, **5C** to **3C**, **5E** to **3C** and **3E** to **3C**. Begin the next star at **1E** and repeat steps 1 and 2 to continue. Work the next row directly below.

Eye

···· LEVEL ····
Intermediate

···· USES ····
Large scale filling

···· METHOD ····
*Square blocks of straight
stitch with open centres,
outlined with back stitch*

···· MATERIALS ····
*Single canvas; thick
thread; embroidery scissors*

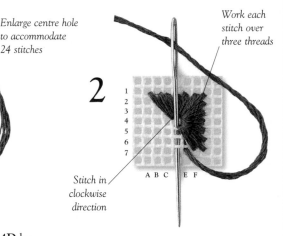

*Enlarge centre hole
to accommodate
24 stitches*

*Work each
stitch over
three threads*

*Stitch in
clockwise
direction*

1 Start at top left. Enlarge the hole at **4D** by carefully twisting the scissor point between the canvas threads. Work two straight stitches from **1A** to **4D** and **1B** to **4D**.

2 Make eleven more stitches into **4D**, starting from **1C, 1D, 1E, 1F, 1G, 2G, 3G, 4G, 5G, 6G** and **7G**. Work the second half as a mirror image of the first, then start the next block at **1G**. Finish off by outlining each square with back stitch (see p.40), worked over one thread.

···· TECHNIQUE VARIATION ····

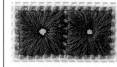

The back stitch outline stitch can be worked in a contrasting colour to create a square grid pattern across the canvas.

Diamond Eye

.... LEVEL ....
Advanced

.... USES ....
*Geometric background or
filling for large areas*

.... METHOD ....
*Straight stitch diamonds
with open centres,
outlined in back stitch*

.... MATERIALS ....
Single canvas; thick thread

*Work each stitch
over three threads*

*Always insert
needle into
same hole*

1 Start at top left with an upright stitch from **1E** to **5E**. Make seven more stitches into the same hole from **2F**, **3G**, **4H**, **5I**, **6H**, **7G**, **8F** and **9E**, then work the second half of the diamond as a mirror image of the first.

2 Work the next block in the same way, starting with **5I** to **9I**, and stitch the next row directly below the first. When the area is complete, outline each diamond with back stitch (see p.40) worked over one thread, to conceal any canvas that may show through.

Fan

.... OTHER NAME ....
Ray stitch

.... LEVEL ....
Easy

.... USES ....
Fine textured filling

.... METHOD ....
*Blocks of radiating stitches,
worked in horizontal rows*

.... MATERIALS ....
Single canvas; thick thread

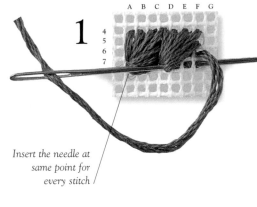

*Insert the needle at
same point for
every stitch*

*Work stitches in
opposite direction
to first row*

1 Starting at bottom left, make an upright stitch from **4A** to **7A**. Work six more stitches into the same hole, from **4B**, **4C**, **4D**, **5D**, **6D** and **7D**, to form a square. Start the next block at **4D** to **7D** and continue working towards the right.

2 Work the next row directly above the first and stitch in the opposite direction, starting at **1G** to **4G**. Repeat steps 1 and 2 to continue.

Looped and Tied Needlepoint Stitches

THIS GROUP INCLUDES some of the most advanced and interesting stitches, which can be used when unusual textures and multi-coloured patterns are required. The looped Rya and Turkey stitches, traditionally used for rugs, are ideal for stitching raised areas within a design and can be trimmed to give a plush finish. The tied and twisted stitches consist of long, straight stitch held down with shorter stitches to give a dense, ridged surface. All the stitches in this section should be worked in a frame on single canvas. Ensure that the thread or yarn used covers all of the background threads.

Rya

.... LEVEL ....
Advanced

.... USES ....
Looped or cut pile stitch for carpet-like texture

.... METHOD ....
Looped stitch worked over knitting needle in horizontal rows

.... MATERIALS ....
Single canvas; thick thread

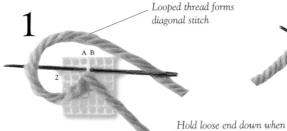

Looped thread forms diagonal stitch

Hold loose end down when pulling needle through

1 Start at bottom left. Take the needle down at **1A** and bring it through at **2A**, leaving a short tail. Insert at **1B** and come back out at **1A**.

2 Pass the needle back under the diagonal loop and pull both ends tightly. Hold the knitting needle below the stitches and take the thread over and under it to form a loop.

3 Repeat steps 1 and 2 to continue, starting the second stitch at **1B**. Work the next and subsequent rows directly above the first. Trim the pile if a tufted effect is required.

Turkey

.... OTHER NAME ....
Ghiordes knot stitch

.... LEVEL ....
Advanced

.... USES ....
Tufted filling; background

.... METHOD ....
Looped stitch, with cut pile

.... MATERIALS ....
Single or rug canvas; thick thread or yarn

Pull needle through below working thread

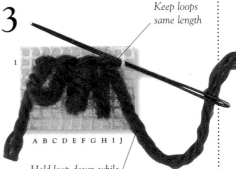

Keep loops same length

Hold loop down while making next stitch

1 Start at bottom left. Insert the needle at **1B** and bring it out at **1A**. Take it down at **1C** and come out again at **1B**.

2 Repeat step 1, starting at **1D**. Leave a loop of thread between the stitches.

3 Continue working towards the right, ensuring the loops are the same length. Work each following row one space above. When the stitching is complete, cut and trim the loops to create a pile.

Houndstooth

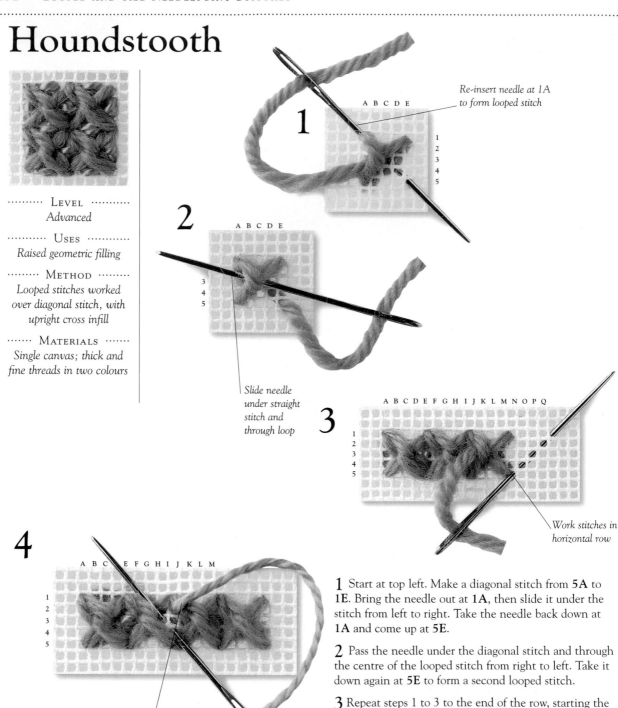

LEVEL
Advanced

USES
Raised geometric filling

METHOD
Looped stitches worked over diagonal stitch, with upright cross infill

MATERIALS
Single canvas; thick and fine threads in two colours

Re-insert needle at 1A to form looped stitch

Slide needle under straight stitch and through loop

Work stitches in horizontal row

Use contrasting pearl thread for cross stitches

1 Start at top left. Make a diagonal stitch from **5A** to **1E**. Bring the needle out at **1A**, then slide it under the stitch from left to right. Take the needle back down at **1A** and come up at **5E**.

2 Pass the needle under the diagonal stitch and through the centre of the looped stitch from right to left. Take it down again at **5E** to form a second looped stitch.

3 Repeat steps 1 to 3 to the end of the row, starting the next stitch at **1I**. Work the next and subsequent rows directly below the first.

4 Using a finer thread in a different colour, work a series of small upright crosses (see p.140) to fill in the spaces between the stitches. Make two straight stitches from **2I** to **4I** and **3H** to **3J**, and continue along the row.

Knitting

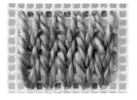

.... LEVEL ....
Easy

.... USES ....
*Filling resembling knitted
stocking stitch*

.... METHOD ....
*Overlapping diagonal
stitches worked vertically
in alternate directions*

.... MATERIALS ....
Single canvas; any thread

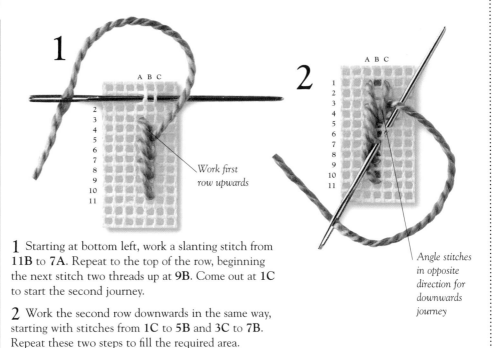

*Work first
row upwards*

*Angle stitches
in opposite
direction for
downwards
journey*

1 Starting at bottom left, work a slanting stitch from
11B to **7A**. Repeat to the top of the row, beginning
the next stitch two threads up at **9B**. Come out at **1C**
to start the second journey.

2 Work the second row downwards in the same way,
starting with stitches from **1C** to **5B** and **3C** to **7B**.
Repeat these two steps to fill the required area.

Old Wheatsheaf

.... LEVEL ....
Advanced

.... USES ....
*In single row as border;
filling for large areas*

.... METHOD ....
*Sheaf filling variation with
contrast interlacing*

.... MATERIALS ....
*Single canvas; any thread
in two contrasting colours*

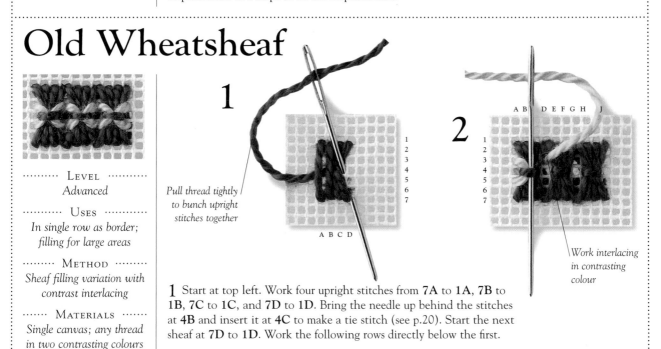

*Pull thread tightly
to bunch upright
stitches together*

*Work interlacing
in contrasting
colour*

1 Start at top left. Work four upright stitches from **7A** to **1A**, **7B** to
1B, **7C** to **1C**, and **7D** to **1D**. Bring the needle up behind the stitches
at **4B** and insert it at **4C** to make a tie stitch (see p.20). Start the next
sheaf at **7D** to **1D**. Work the following rows directly below the first.

2 Using the second thread, bring the needle up at **3A**. Slide it
downwards under the tie stitch, and insert at **5A**. Come up at **3D**,
pass the needle under the tie stitch again, and take it down at **5D**.
Lace each sheaf in the same way.

Tied Gobelin

····· OTHER NAMES ·····
Knotted stitch

········· LEVEL ·········
Intermediate

········· USES ·········
Filling with ridged texture

········ METHOD ········
*Horizontal rows of
interlocking tied diagonal
stitches*

······ MATERIALS ······
Single canvas; any thread

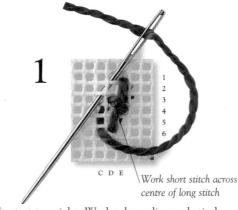

*Work short stitch across
centre of long stitch*

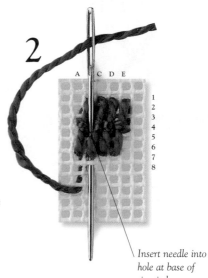

*Insert needle into
hole at base of
tie stitch*

1 Start at top right. Work a long diagonal stitch
from **6D** to **1E**, crossed by a short stitch from **4E** to
3D. Make the next pair of stitches from **6C** to **1D**
and **3C** to **4D**, and continue working to the left.

2 The next row is stitched in the opposite direction.
Work the first two stitches from **9A** to **4B** and **7B** to
6A and repeat to the end of the row. Repeat these
two rows to fill the required area.

French

········· LEVEL ·········
Intermediate

········· USES ·········
*Textured, ridged filling or
background*

········ METHOD ········
*Pairs of tied upright
stitches worked in
horizontal rows*

······ MATERIALS ······
Single canvas; any thread

*Work both upright
stitches in same holes*

*Work second row
into spaces between
first pairs of stitches*

1 Start at top left. Make an upright stitch from **7B** to
1B held down by a tie stitch (see p.20) from **4B** to **4A**.
Work a second upright stitch from **7B** to **1B** and anchor
it with a tie stitch from **4C** to **4B**. Continue making
pairs of tied stitches to the end of the row.

2 Work the next row in the opposite direction, starting
with an upright stitch from **10E** to **4E** and a tie stitch
from **7E** to **7F**. Repeat these two rows to continue.

Pineapple

········ LEVEL ········
Advanced

········· USES ··········
*Two-coloured geometric
filling for large areas*

········ METHOD ········
*Tied cross stitches worked
over upright Gobelin stitch*

······ MATERIALS ·······
*Single canvas; any thread
in two colours*

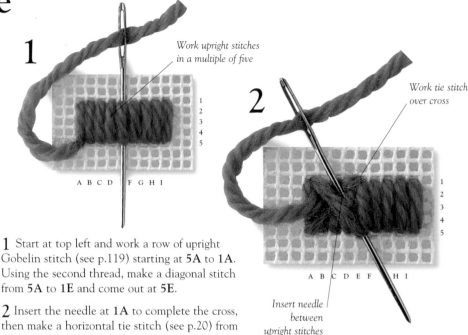

*Work upright stitches
in a multiple of five*

*Work tie stitch
over cross*

*Insert needle
between
upright stitches*

1 Start at top left and work a row of upright Gobelin stitch (see p.119) starting at **5A** to **1A**. Using the second thread, make a diagonal stitch from **5A** to **1E** and come out at **5E**.

2 Insert the needle at **1A** to complete the cross, then make a horizontal tie stitch (see p.20) from **3B** to **3D**. Continue working crosses along the row, then work subsequent rows directly below.

Arrow

········ LEVEL ········
Intermediate

········· USES ··········
*Textured filling; in single
rows as a border*

········ METHOD ········
*Angled variation of sheaf
filling, worked in rows*

······ MATERIALS ·······
Single canvas; any thread

*Work upright stitches
over four threads*

*Pull thread up
tightly to draw
stitches to right*

1 Starting in the top left corner, work three upright stitches from **5A** to **1A**, **5B** to **1B**, and **5C** to **1C**. Bring the needle out at **3D** and slide it under the three stitches from right to left.

2 Take the needle back down at **3D** and bring it out at **5C**, ready to make the next upright stitch. Repeat steps 1 and 2 to continue, and work the following rows directly below the first.

Index

Acknowledgments

Author's acknowledgments

No writer can work in isolation, and this book would not have been possible without the joint skills of the art and editorial teams at both Dorling Kindersley and C&B Packaging. I would like to extend my thanks to all the many colleagues and friends who have contributed their experience and commitment over the past year.

I am indebted to Samantha Gray, who first suggested my name to the publishers. Nigel Duffield, Mary Lindsay, Sarah Hall, and Cathy Shilling at DK have given me every encouragement, along with their invaluable guidance and enthusiasm, from the outset.

Managing editor Kate Yeates has been my mainstay: her dedication and constant good humour have helped me through to the end of the project. Special thanks also to Roger Bristow and Helen Collins at C&B Packaging for their invaluable creative input, to Sam Lloyd for patiently photographing all the many stitch samples and to Heather Dewhurst for editing my text so meticulously.

Lis Gunner embroidered my designs for the chapter openers and gave me useful advice about stitching.

Debbie Kilby of Anything Left-Handed (Tel: 0208 770 3727) advised me on techniques for left-handed workers.

Finally, I must thank my husband Jonathan Hayden-Williams for always being there for me, and my sister Emma Ganderton and father Colin Ganderton for their unfailing support, for which I am ever grateful.

Dorling Kindersley would like to thank the following:

DMC Creative World Ltd for supplying the needles, pearl cottons, tapestry yarns, evenweave linen and canvas used to create the step-by-step examples and finished stitch samples. Thanks in particular to Cara Ackerman for all her help. For further information about DMC products contact them at: Pullman Road, Wigston, Leicestershire, LE18 2DY. Tel: 0116 281 1040.

Additional assistance

Editorial: Nicola Munro
Design: Cathy Shilling
Administration: Christopher Gordon
Additional Photography: (p.12)
Andy Crawford, Steve Gorton